Undergraduate Topics in Computer Science

Undergraduate Topics in Computer Science (UTiCS) delivers high-quality instructional content for undergraduates studying in all areas of computing and information science. From core foundational and theoretical material to final-year topics and applications, UTiCS books take a fresh, concise, and modern approach and are ideal for self-study or for a one- or two-semester course. The texts are all authored by established experts in their fields, reviewed by an international advisory board, and contain numerous examples and problems. Many include fully worked solutions.

More information about this series at http://www.springer.com/series/7592

Alan Holt · Chi-Yu Huang

Embedded Operating Systems

A Practical Approach

Second Edition

Alan Holt
Zeetta Networks
Bristol
UK

Chi-Yu Huang
GE Aviation Systems
Cheltenham
UK

ISSN 1863-7310   ISSN 2197-1781   (electronic)
Undergraduate Topics in Computer Science
ISBN 978-3-319-72976-3   ISBN 978-3-319-72977-0   (eBook)
https://doi.org/10.1007/978-3-319-72977-0

Library of Congress Control Number: 2017962063

This Springer imprint is published by the registered company Springer International
Publishing AG part of Springer Nature
The registered company address is: Gewerbestrasse 11, 6330 Cham, Switzerland

*In memory of Marjorie Rose Holt and
Siou-yìn Zheng Huang*

Preface to the Second Edition

Since the first edition, operating systems and the software packages that are bundled with them have progressed. Nowadays, 64-bit desktop/laptop computers are commonplace. This was not the case when the first edition was published. There are some 64-bit architectures that are used for embedded platforms but 32-bit (or less) machines are still prevalent. Whereas in the first edition we would be building software for 32-bit targets on 32-bit hosts, we now need to *cross-compile* on 64-bit hosts. In the real-world, this is what would be done but it does add a level of complexity to the practical exercises in this book.

Furthermore, the work examples in this book have software dependencies (utilities and shared libraries). Not only that, particular versions of these dependencies are required. In the first edition, we addressed this issue by recommending the reader use the same operating system platform that the authors used to develop the exercises. This is not really practical, not least for the authors themselves given that dependency versions have moved on since the first edition.

For these reasons, we have introduced some new technologies in this edition. First, we make use of virtual machines. We used virtual machine technology, such as user mode Linux (UML), in the first edition as a means of testing operating system builds. In this edition, we use VirtualBox so that we can build software on a (virtualized) 32-bit platform even though our host machine may be 64-bit. This obviates the need to cross-compile.

We rely heavily on Linux container technology to build software, namely, *Docker*. Docker is a container system which enables us to replicate environments and ensure commonality between the authors' and the reader's respective development platforms. As well as helping us to build operating systems, it is also useful for testing. We dedicate a whole new chapter to Docker and its uses as a means of introducing the technology.

Bristol, UK   Alan Holt
Cheltenham, UK   Chi-Yu Huang

Preface to the First Edition

Most people are aware of the mainstream operating systems such as Microsoft's Windows or Apple's macOS. This is because these are the operating systems that they directly interact with on their personal computers. However, personal computers rarely operate in isolation nowadays.

Many computing applications require *online* access. Access to the Internet relies on many computing systems, for example, Ethernet switches, packet routers, wireless access points, and DHCP and DNS servers. Unlike personal computers, network infrastructure equipments perform dedicated tasks and are often described as "embedded systems".

The term "embedded system" covers a range of computing systems. It derives from computing systems that are *embedded* within some larger device, for example, as part of a car's engine management system. The term has broadened to cover stand-alone systems too. Nor is it limited to network infrastructure systems or consumer goods such as satellite navigation devices. The term "embedded system" is applied to devices which are small and have limited resources (relative to a personal computer). Mobile devices such as smartphones and tablets are, therefore, described as embedded devices, even though their function closely resembles a personal computer. Nevertheless, an embedded system needs an operating system specific to its needs, for example,

- Small form factor.
- Low processing power and small memory.
- Reduced power consumption for battery longevity.
- Support for real-time applications.

There are many embedded operating systems available; however, in this book we confine our discussion to the GNU/Linux operating system. GNU/Linux is not exclusively an embedded operating system and is used on personal computers and servers just like Windows and macOS. However, due to its open-source nature it can be easily adapted to many environments. For this reason, GNU/Linux systems have gained considerable popularity in the embedded system market.

That is not to say that GNU/Linux is a panacea for embedded systems and there are many excellent alternatives. Nevertheless, there are some good reasons for choosing GNU/Linux:

- GNU/Linux is open source and is freely available.
- Due to its open-source nature, GNU/Linux is highly customizable so we can build bespoke systems specific to our needs.
- It is widely used for embedded systems.
- GNU/Linux, like its Unix predecessor, was used extensively in education to teach operating systems.
- While the subject of the book is embedded operating systems, our choice of GNU/Linux means it could be used as a text for a more general course on operating systems.

Operating systems is a diverse subject area and there are many books on the subject and of GNU/Linux alone. A variety of topics are covered including the kernel, administration, networking, wireless, high-performance computing, and systems programming (to name but a few). There are even books on GNU/Linux embedded systems.

However, we felt there was a gap in the literature which described the components parts of an operating system and how they worked together. We address these issues in this book by adopting a practical approach. The procedure for building each component of the operating system, namely, the bootloader, kernel, filesystem, shared libraries, start-up scripts, configuration files, and system utilities, from its source code, is described in detail. By the end of this book, the reader will be able to build a fully functional GNU/Linux embedded operating system.

This book is not an introductory text on operating systems, rather it is aimed at undergraduate/graduate level students and industry professionals.

Acknowledgements

The authors would like to thank Dr. Adrian Davies and Justin Johnstone for their valuable contributions to this book.

Contents

List of Figures

List of Tables

Introduction

Most people are familiar with general purpose computing devices, such as desktops and laptops. Their use is common-place and supports a wide variety of applications, many of which involve a wider access to distributed applications over the Internet (electronic mail, social media etc.). Users interact with general purpose computers directly through keyboards, mice and monitor screens. There are many consumer devices, such as mobile phones, tablet computers and satellite navigation devices, that are classified as embedded devices. They support user interaction through touch screens, microphones, audio speakers and accelerometers.

Nevertheless, many embedded systems operate in the background with little or no direct human interaction. Embedded computer systems are used extensively throughout our technological society.

As we look to the future we should contemplate an *Internet-of-things* (IoT). IoT predicts the attachment of computing devices (with network capabilities) to *objects*. The attributes of such an object can be monitored and digitised by its associated computing device which are then relayed (over a network) to a remote system for analysis.

A precursor to the Internet-of-things is smart energy metering like that of 3E-Houses [1]. Energy monitoring devices were installed in social housing to record energy consumption in domestic homes and the data was transmitted over the Internet to a central database. This data was analysed and fed back to the participants of the project to increase their awareness of their energy usage. The hope was, that through this feedback mechanism, people would reduce their energy consumption and CO_2 footprint.

© Springer International Publishing AG, part of Springer Nature 2018
A. Holt and C.-Y. Huang, *Embedded Operating Systems*, Undergraduate
Topics in Computer Science, https://doi.org/10.1007/978-3-319-72977-0_1

1.1   An Overview of Operating Systems

Operating systems are software components dedicated to the management of the
computer system's hardware. Most computer systems (embedded or otherwise) operate under the control of an operating system. Unix-like operating systems, such as
GNU/Linux, comprise a kernel, software libraries and a number of utility programs.
The diagram in Fig. 1.1 shows the operating system architecture. A piece of software
called a bootloader is also required to start the kernel when the computer system is
powered. We discuss the bootloader in more detail in Chap. 2.

The kernel is a program that manages the resources of a computer system. It
allocates these resources between separate processes in a controlled way. Processes
are computer programs under execution and may be initiated by different users.
Resources are, therefore, not just allocated amongst processes, but also amongst
users. What distinguishes the kernel from the rest of the operating system software,
is the processor privilege level at which the respective code is executed. Most modern processors support multiple privilege levels. Intel 386 processors, for example,
support four privilege levels. GNU/Linux only uses two, level 0 (the most privileged)
for the executing kernel code and level 3 (least privileged) for running user code.

The reason for these different privilege levels is to prevent user code from directly
accessing certain hardware resources. For example, I/O port instructions can only be
accessed by kernel code. Clearly, user processes require access to peripheral devices
(I/O port instructions) on the computer system. A process can *context switch* into
kernel mode by issuing a software trap. In kernel mode, a process can access hardware
via the kernel's own subsystems. Access to hardware is, therefore, controlled by the
kernel. Functions of the kernel can be characterised below:

Process management: Computer systems store a number of programs in their
   memory. These programs may be part of the operating system's utilities or software written by a user as an application. A program under execution is called a
   process. The system may execute multiple processes concurrently. The process
   management system gives the illusion of processes running simultaneously, typically, by giving each process a *time slice* of the CPU (or CPUs). A scheduler
   makes the decision as to which process is allocated a time slice. A process may
   have its execution suspended and resumed several times before it terminates.

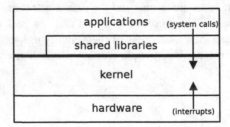

Fig. 1.1 Operating system overview

Memory management: Memory management is a complex function. In order to manage memory efficiently and effectively, the kernel implements *virtual memory*. Virtual memory gives the appearance that a process has more memory than it actually has (or even, more than the entire system has). The virtual and physical memory are divided into *pages*. With paged memory a virtual address is divided into two parts, namely, a virtual page frame number plus an offset into the page. When a virtual memory location is referenced, the virtual page frame is translated into a physical page frame number. The offset is then used to identify the specific memory location within the page.

Filesystem: Persistent data is stored in files which in turn are organised in directories. The filesystem provides the functions and data structures required to manage files and directories (as well as other files objects) within a disk partition.

Device management: In addition to the CPU and main memory, a computer system will comprise a variety of peripheral devices. For example, disk drives, network interfaces, input/output devices etc. Device drivers are pieces of software within the kernel that control the devices.

1.2 Overview of Embedded Systems

Embedded systems are hard to define. The problem lies in the fact there are exceptions to any rules one may conceive. While it is not easy to find a characteristic that is exclusive to embedded systems we shall examine a few below:

A Subsystem of a device or machine: Such systems are *embedded* within a more sophisticated device or machine, an engine management system of a car or microprocessor within an appliance, for example. Given this definition, we can view a general processing computer as being made up of a number of embedded systems. In addition to the CPU and main memory, general processing computers also include bus controllers, disk controllers, network interfaces and video controllers. All of which could be considered embedded systems in their own right. Furthermore, there are numerous *non-subsystem* examples of embedded systems, WiFi access-points, network routers, set-top boxes, for example.

Dedicated application: Embedded systems are largely designed to perform a specific task such as monitoring a temperature sensor or controlling a valve. In the case of consumer electronics devices may perform multiple tasks. Modern mobile phones are rarely limited to just making telephone calls. Many are described as *smart* phones and can support a plethora of applications. Given the increase in the power and sophistication of embedded devices it is difficult to distinguish them from general processing systems.

Small footprint: A small footprint is a typical characteristic of embedded systems. This is usually driven by the task it has to perform.

Low power consumption: Many embedded systems are battery powered and need to conserve energy consumption. Such systems may be static or mobile, either way they operate at a distance from any mains power. There are obvious exemptions to this rule. High speed routers and switches, for example, have powerful processors for forwarding high volumes of network packets. Consequently energy consumption will be high and mains supplied.

Low processing power and memory: This is somewhat a corollary of the characteristic above. Whereas, in the past, embedded systems were almost exclusively based on specially designed hardware, it is possible nowadays to develop embedded systems on commercial off-the-shelf (COTS) hardware.

Real-Time systems: Real-time systems are systems that must respond to events within strict time constraints. The term "real-time system" is sometimes used synonymously with embedded systems. Real-time systems are almost always dedicated to a single application and can be categorised as embedded systems. However, not all embedded systems support real-time applications.

Requires specially designed operating system: This characteristic may have been true in the past when embedded system had limited processing and memory resources. It is still true to some extent but the increase in processor speed and memory size means that operating systems that run on general purpose computing platforms can be used on embedded systems. The Linux kernel for an embedded system will almost certainly need to be customised to work on the target platform (but this is true of any computer system). For devices that lack memory management units (MMUs) there is a separate Linux kernel branch called uClinux. Systems that need to support real-time applications need a real-time kernel. The vanilla Linux kernel does not support real-time. There is a real-time version of Linux, namely, RTLinux which has an RTOS (real-time operating system)microkernel.

Interact with the physical world Physical computing: is a branch of computing concerned with sensing and responding to the analogue world. This application is considered the domain of embedded systems.

Single board computer: Entire computer systems can be built on a single printed circuit board (PCB). The PCB includes the CPU memory and peripheral devices. Such systems are called single board computers (SBCs) and are well suited to embedded system platforms. It is possible to go beyond single *board* computers with system on a chip (SoC). This format too, lends itself to embedded system design.

The distinction between an embedded system and a general processing system is somewhat blurred. The Raspberry Pi for example, fits many of the criteria above, yet is primarily designed to function as a general processing computer. Given that it shares many characteristics of an embedded system, it is being used extensively for embedded applications.

We do not intend to get overly concerned with strict definitions of embedded systems in this book. Our focus is on the core components of an embedded operating system. For this reason, we omit graphical user interfaces and sophisticated user input devices. Nor are we concerned with the processing of multimedia such as audio and video. We accept that consumer electronics systems, which are considered to be embedded systems, do support sophisticated GUIs (touch screens, for example) and multimedia, nevertheless, these components are outside the scope of this book.

We complete this section with a list of (typical) embedded system applications. This is by no means an exhaustive list but gives some idea of the scope of the subject area:

- Consumer electronics: cameras, mobile phones portable gaming consoles, satellite navigation and GPS handsets.
- Automotive electronics: cruise control and navigation.
- Communications equipment: base stations, network routers and wireless access-points.
- Factory automation equipment: robots, sensor and inventory control systems
- Office automation equipment: scanners, photocopiers and printers.
- Home automation: security systems, temperature control smart meters.

1.3   Brief History of Linux and GNU

Linux is a *Unix-like* operating system developed by Linus Torvalds. To understand the origins of Linux, we present a brief history of the Unix operating system and some of its derivatives.

Unix was developed in 1969 by Ken Thompson, Dennis Ritchie, and Douglas McIlroy at AT&T Bell Laboratories. Unix is a multi-user, time-sharing operating system. It was first developed for medium-sized computers, but has been ported to personal computers and super computers. The reason that Unix was so portable, was that it was developed in a machine independent language. Typically, the development of an operating system was tightly coupled to the computer system it was designed for. This was because operating systems were written in machine dependent languages (assembler or machine code). While the first versions of Unix were developed in assembler, later versions were developed in the high-level language C [2] (also conceived by the Bell Laboratories). Unix System III was released in 1982, followed by Unix System V in 1983 which AT&T was able to market after its divestiture.

BSD (Berkeley Software Distribution) Unix was developed by the Computer Systems Research Group (CSRG) at the University of California, Berkeley. The initial BSD Unix was an augmentation of the Bell Labs Unix. There have been a number of Unix-derivatives based on BSD. For example, SunOS from Sun Microsystems is a version of BSD Unix (one of the co-founders of Sun, Bill Joy was a BSD developer). Later, SunOS was re-branded as Solaris and was based on System V Release 4 (see below).

As Unix matured, CSRG no longer considered BSD Unix a research interest and terminated its development. A number of Unix-like, open-source operating systems descended from BSD, namely, FreeBSD [3,4], NetBSD, and OpenBSD [5]. Darwin, the macOS kernel, is based on the Mach kernel and is derived from the BSD implementation of Unix in Nextstep. Nextstep was the object-oriented operating system developed by Steve Jobs when he was at NeXT after leaving Apple in 1985.

In 1987, AT&T (in collaboration with Sun Microsystems) merged System V release 3, BSD and Xenix to form System V Release 4 (SVR4).

Attempts to standardise Unix in the late 80s and early 90s gave rise to the Unix wars. This adversely affected its acceptance in the market. The alliance between AT&T and Sun Microsystems concerned many other Unix vendors. This gave rise to two opposing factions, the X/Open consortium and OSF (Open System Foundation).

In 1991, AT&T "spun off" its Unix System Laboratories (USL) and Unix when it sold the Unix operating system. The following year, the Novell Corporation signed a letter of intent to purchase USL and Unix. The transaction was completed in 1993. The same year, Novell sold its entire Unix business to the Santa Cruz Operation (SCO).

The GNU (GNU is Not Unix) project was initiated by Richard Stallman to produce a free Unix-like operating system. The intended kernel for the GNU system was the Hurd kernel. Hurd stands for "HIRD of Unix-Replacing Daemons" and HIRD stands for HURD of Interfaces Representing Depth. Despite the wealth on recursive (and circular) acronyms, HURD never became the GNU kernel due to its slow development. The BSD kernel was considered GNU but was ruled out due to the AT&T lawsuit against BDSI.

Minix is a Unix-like operating system developed by Andrew S. Tanenbaum. Tanenbaum developed Minux for educational purposes. Released under the BSD license, Minix is free and open source software. It was Minix that largely inspired Linus Torvalds to develop the Linux kernel. Linux was initially released under Torvalds' own license but later it was released under GNU General Public License. Making the Linux source code available to the wider community meant others could contribute to its development. Development of the GNU software was also required to integrate it with the Linux Kernel. GNU/Linux operating systems are disseminated as *distributions*. Table 1.1 shows some of the popular distributions in use to today.

1.4   GNU/Linux as an Embedded Operating System

GNU/Linux was not developed specifically for the embedded system market but, given that it can easily be customised, it is well suited to embedded projects. There are a number of advantages to using GNU/Linux as an operating system for embedded systems:

- GNU/Linux is open source, therefore, there are no licence fees.
- The software is fairly mature and stable.
- There is a large community of developers.
- Access to the source code means that modifications can be made to suit the application.

Table 1.1 GNU/Linux distributions

Name	Root	Provider	Comment
Debian	–	The Debian project	
Fedora	–	Community	Red Hat sponsored
Slackware	–	Slackware	The oldest distribution
openSuse	–	Suse	
Gentoo Linux	–	Gentoo Foundation	Source based distribution
Chrome OS	Gentoo	Google	Google's commercial Linux
Red Hat Enterprise Linux	Fedora	Red Hat	
Oracle Linux	Fedora/RHEL	Oracle	
Ubuntu	Debian	Canonical	
Mint	Debian/Ubuntu	Community	
Centos	RHEL	Community Enterprise O/S	

There are some disadvantages of course. The Linux kernel is large and complex as it is designed, primarily, for multi-user, timesharing environments. The kernel also lacks support for real-time which is a requirement of some embedded applications. There are a couple of solutions to this limitation. There are a number of patches (such as PREEMPT-RT) which enable real-time support within the Linux kernel. Also, there is RTLinux which is an RTOS microkernel that runs the Linux kernel as a pre-emptive process.

The current Linux kernel is designed to work with a memory management unit (MMU) which many embedded platforms lack. μCLinux is a Linux kernel fork designed to work with processors which do not have an MMU. There are a number of GNU/Linux distributions specifically designed for embedded systems, a few are listed below:

Openwrt: Linksys used firmware for the WRT54G series of routers based upon code that was licensed under GPL (GNU public license). Linksys, therefore, had to release their modified code, enabling community developers to produce new versions of the firmware. The Openwrt project originated from the initial development. Openwrt supports a wide variety of process architectures. It uses the ipkg package management system. We discuss Openwrt in more detail in Chap. 9.

LEDE: Linux embedded development environment (LEDE) is a fork of Openwrt.

Arch Linux: The Arch Linux distribution is primarily for i686 and x86-64 architectures but there is also a distribution for ARM processors. It uses the pacman for package management, which was developed specifically for Arch Linux.

Angstrom: The Angstrom distribution supports a variety of embedded devices. The
    distribution derives from a number of projects, namely, OpenZaurus, OpenEm-
    bedded, and OpenSIMpad. Angstrom is used on the BeagleBone and BeagleBoard
    platforms. The package management system for Angstorm is opkg.
Android: Android is designed for tablets and smart phones. It was developed by
    Google and the Open Handset Alliance.

1.5   Conventions Used in This Book

We use a GNU/Linux platform throughout this book, namely, Ubuntu 16.04. In
computing literature it is conventional to use the term "Linux" to refer to the operating
system. Linux, however, is only kernel. The rest of the operating software (or most
of it at least) is GNU. We use the term GNU/Linux in recognition of both the kernel
developers and the developers of other essential components of the operating system.
Sometimes we use the term "Unix" when referring to a feature that is common to all
Unix and Unix-like operating systems such as GNU/Linux. We use the term "Linux"
to refer to the entire operating system (rather than just the kernel) only when it is
used that way by others.

Most of the examples are performed on a general purpose Intel 386 based platform running Ubuntu 16.04 LTS. We use a number of technologies, such as Linux
containers and virtual machine, in order to ensure commonality between reader and
author environments.

Some examples are performed on actual embedded GNU/Linux systems. Often,
this necessitates running commands on both an embedded system and a host machine.
We even run commands in virtual machines, Docker containers and Linux namespaces. The text explains which commands are run on which platform but, in order to
make it clear, we use different command-line prompts to distinguish between them.
A single dollar sign, $ is used to denote the command-line for a general host machine.
The $ also means that commands are run as a regular user. If the prompt is a # then
commands are run as superuser. Commands are seldom run while logged in to the
superuser account, instead we use the sudo utility when we need to run commands
with superuser privileges.

Most of the examples given in this book are from the GNU/Linux command-
line. Throughout we assume Bash as the default shell. Input to and output from
the command-line is in a monospaced font. The example below shows the date
command entered at the command-line prompt ($). Below this line is the output of
the command:

```
$ date
Mon Sep  9 14:36:51 BST 2013
```

Names of files (including absolute and relative pathnames) are highlighted in italic, */etc/hostname*, for example.

1.6 Book Outline

This book is organised as follows:

Chapter 2: Overview of GNU/Linux. In this chapter we give a brief overview of the GNU/Linux system. We introduce the components of the system, such as the bootloader, kernel and filesystem. We also cover process management, process input/output and the process environment.

Chapter 3: Containers. In this chapter we look at containers and the underlying kernel technology upon which they are based. There are a number of Linux container systems but we confine our discussion to Docker. We use Docker in later chapters to build and test embedded system software.

Chapter 4: The Filesystem. Access to persistent storage is supported through the *filesystem*. GNU/Linux supports many filesystem types by using a virtual filesystem (VFS). In this chapter we discuss GNU/Linux filesystems in detail.

Chapter 5: Building an Embedded System (first pass). In this chapter we describe how to build an embedded system using the debootstrap utility. We build the system to run under a virtual machine. The virtualisation technology we use is user mode Linux (UML).

Chapter 6: Building an Embedded System (second pass). We build an embedded system to run natively on an actual processor. We build all the system components from the source code, including the kernel, bootloader, shared libraries and Unix utilities. We also create the boot scripts and system configuration files.

Chapter 7: Compiler Toolchains. In this chapter we introduce the concept of the compiler toolchain (or just toolchain). Compilers translate instructions from a high-level programming language into machine dependent binary executable' code. The "compiler" is rarely a single program, but rather a suite of programs, hence a *toolchain*. Embedded devices are, typically, low in CPU and memory, thus, running compiler toolchains on the actual target can be impractical. For this reason, *cross* compiler toolchains are required to build software for a particular target architecture but run on a platform of a different architecture.

Chapter 8: Embedded ARM Devices. In this chapter we look at two ARM based platforms: BeagleBone and Raspberry Pi. The BeagleBone and BeagleBone Black are part of the BeagleBoard series of single-board computers produced by Texas Instruments and Digi-Key. They are aimed at the educational and hobbiest market. The BeagleBones are shipped with the Angstrom GNU/Linux distribution.
The Raspberry Pi was designed as inexpensive PC and aimed at the educational market but its small form factor makes it ideal for embedded system use. The

Raspberry Pi can run a number of GNU/Linux distributions as well as a few
non-GNU/Linux operating systems.

Chapter 9:   Openwrt. Openwrt is a GNU/Linux distribution for embedded systems.
Openwrt originally came out of development of the firmware for the Linksys
WRT54G home router series but the project quickly expanded to many other
systems. In this chapter we focus on two particular devices that run the Openwrt
operating system, namely the OMxP Open-mesh devices and the Dragino MS14
series. We show how to build Openwrt firmware images for both of these units.

References

1. Holt A (2013) Get smart. Linux Magazine, 5, pp 47–51
2. Kernighan BW, Ritchie DM (1978) The C programming language. Prentice-Hall Software Series,
   New Jersey
3. Greg L (2003) The complete FreeBSD. O'Reilly
4. Kirk McKusick M, Neville-Neil GV (2004) The design and implementation of the FreeBSD
   operating system. Pearson Education
5. Lucas M (2003) Absolute OpenBSD: Unix for the practical paranoid. No Starch Press Series,
   No Starch Press

Overview of GNU/Linux

2

The GNU/Linux operating system software comprises four components:

- Bootloader
- Kernel
- Shared libraries
- System commands and utilities

A full GNU/Linux distribution will also include a large collection of application software (email clients, web browsers, database management systems, compilers, for example) but for the purposes of this chapter, we focus on the four components listed above.

When a computer powers up, the bootloader is the first piece of software to execute (after any firmware power-on self-tests) and is primarily responsible for loading the kernel. Due to space constraints, the bootloader may be separated into stages. The first stage is, typically, small and located in a specific area of system's disk (or other non-volatile memory). The first stage bootloader loads the next stage of the bootloader. Additional stages of the bootloader are located within a filesystem (which need not be the root filesystem).

Control is passed to the kernel once it has been loaded. The kernel initialises various systems and then creates the first process (called init) which in turn, starts the system's *daemon* processes including services that allow users to login.

Shared libraries are collections of object code that are linked into programs at either compile time (static libraries) or run time (dynamic libraries). There are a number of benefits to shared libraries. Library code can be modified and re-compiled without having to re-compile any application software that uses it. Conversely, if

© Springer International Publishing AG, part of Springer Nature 2018   11
A. Holt and C.-Y. Huang, *Embedded Operating Systems*, Undergraduate
Topics in Computer Science, https://doi.org/10.1007/978-3-319-72977-0_2

the application software is re-compiled, it is not necessary to re-compile any of the libraries. Furthermore, dynamic libraries reduce memory usage. Only one copy of a dynamic library need reside in memory even though many running programs (processes) may use it.

A GNU/Linux system requires at least one filesystem, called the root filesystem. Much of the operating system software resides on this filesystem. The kernel and bootloader sometimes reside on a separate (small) filesystem called the boot filesystem. One of the reasons for this is that, some bootloaders only support certain filesystems types, which may not include the filesystem type of the root filesystem (like a native Linux filesystem).

In this chapter we present an overview of a GNU/Linux system and discuss its component parts. We also look at process management and introduce some useful tools and features that we will use in later chapters.

2.1 The Bootloader

The bootloader is a piece of software that runs when the system boots up and is responsible for loading the kernel (amongst other things). In this section we describe the operation of the bootloader. For convenience, we assume an IBM-compatible PC system. The boot process for other architectures may vary.

The code for the bootloader (or at least the first part of the bootloader) is stored in the *boot sector* of a disk (which is flagged as the boot disk). This bootsector also stores the partition table. The bootloader is either on the first block of the disk or in first block of a partition. In PC nomenclature, there are two types of boot sector:

- Master boot record (MBR): the boot sector at the start of a partitioned disk.
- Volume boot record (VBR): the boot sector at the start of a non-partitioned disk or at the start of a partition.

The MBR may contain a bootloader for booting a kernel *or* it may contain a boot manager that *chain loads* bootstrap code in a VBR (on one of the partitions). For the purpose of this explanation, we will assume the bootloader in the MBR loads the kernel directly.

Before the bootloader can be executed, it has to be loaded from disk into memory. On IBM-compatible systems this is done by the basic input output system (BIOS). When the CPU is powered on it executes a jump instruction which passes control to the BIOS code in ROM. The BIOS initialises some of the hardware and then performs a power-on self-test (POST).

If the POST passes, the BIOS loads the content of the MBR (the bootloader code and the partition table) from the boot disk at a specific memory location. It then jumps to the first instruction of the bootloader. The bootloader loads the kernel into memory and passes control to it. As there is only 440 bytes available for bootstrap code, there is a limit to what the MBR resident bootloader can do. For this reason, the MBR bootloader loads a second stage bootloader from the hard disk (which does not have the same size restrictions as the MBR bootloader). Additional bootloader stages may be loaded before the kernel itself is loaded.

There are a number of bootloaders available for booting Linux kernels. A few of the popular ones are described below:

LILO: The Linux loader (LILO) was the default loader for GNU/Linux distributions in the early years. LILO has been superseded by GRUB as the default bootloader.

GNU GRUB: Grand unified bootloader is a sophisticated bootloader that is used extensively with GNU/Linux systems. It comes in two flavours, GRUB 1 and GRUB 2 though there is no longer any development for GRUB 1 and it is being phased out in favour of GRUB 2.

SYSLINUX: SYSLINUX is a lightweight bootloader which is ideal for GNU/Linux embedded systems. SYSLINUX can only boot from FAT and NTFS filesystems. There are a number of SYSLINUX derivatives:

- ISOLINUX is a bootloader for ISO 9660 CD-ROM filesystems.
- PXELINUX is a bootloader for booting over the network from a remote server. This is based on the preboot execution environment (PXE) system.
- EXTLINUX is a version of SYSLINUX which can boot from ext2, ext3 and ext4 filesystems.

Das U-Boot: Das U-Boot (universal bootloader) is an open source boot loader specifically for embedded devices. It is available for various architectures, for example: ARM, AVR32, MIPS, PPC, x86, 68k, Nios, and MicroBlaze.

2.2 The Kernel

The Linux kernel operates between the computer system hardware and user-space applications. It manages the hardware (CPU, memory and peripheral devices), and runs user programs. Computer systems may be shared by multiple users so the kernel must also ensure the integrity of the system and enforce security. Linus Torvalds began development of the Linux kernel in 1991 but since then a large community of developers have contributed to its development. Indeed, the majority of development is done by this community rather than Torvalds himself. Nevertheless Torvalds maintains an active role in the development and has the final say regarding new features. The Linux kernel is released under the GNU General Public License version 2 (GPLv2) The source code for the Linux kernel can be downloaded from [1]. The kernel source directory is divided into subdirectories, a brief summary of the structure is outlined below:

linux/kernel: The core kernel code.

linux/include: Contains header files for both kernel and user applications.

linux/arch: Architecture dependent parts of the kernel.

linux/drivers: Device driver code.

linux/fs: Code the virtual file system (VFS) and the physical filesystems.

linux/init: Architecture independent boot code and the initial entry point to kernel.

linux/ipc: Source code for interprocess communication (IPC) methods, namely, semaphores, shared memory and messages.

linux/mm: Memory management functions, namely, allocation of memory, memory mapping and paging/swapping.

linux/scripts: Supporting scripts for kernel configuration, patching and documentation.

The Linux kernel resides in the */boot* directory (typically) in either of two file formats: zImage or bzImage (big zImage). The kernel image comprises two parts, a compressed part preceded by an uncompressed header. The bootloader loads the kernel image into memory and passes control to the first instruction in the uncompressed header. This part of the kernel runs in real mode (for i386 processors). After completing some initialisation tasks it switches to protected mode. The kernel relocates itself (several times) in memory before decompressing the compressed part of the image. Control is then passed to this part of the kernel. This thread of execution eventually becomes the idle process which executes when there are no user processes on the run queue. The kernel creates the first user process and assigns it a process ID (PID) of 1. The init program code is located and executed in this process.

The Linux kernel is highly customisable with many configuration options (such as device drivers). These options can either be built into the kernel image *or* as a loadable module. If the latter is used, an option in the kernel needs to be set to support loadable modules. Modules can be added to, or removed from the kernel dynamically. The benefit of this is, they do not need to resident in memory if they are not actually required. Embedded systems tend to have fixed hardware configurations and, therefore, a set number of device drivers which must be loaded at all times. In which case they may as well be built into the kernel.

2.3   The Init Process

The init process is the first user space process. All processes running on the system are descendants of the init process (though not necessarily direct descendants). There are a number of versions of init. In this book we restrict our discussions to the System V version (Sysvinit). The System V initialisation procedure adopts the concept of *runlevels*. Runlevels determine the state of the machine after boot and thus the services that are started or terminated. Examples of operating system modes defined by runlevels are:

Table 2.1 Unix System V runlevels used by the Linux standard base

ID	Name	Description
0	Halt	System shutdown
1	Single-user mode	Single-user mode for administrative tasks
2	Multi-user mode	Multi-user mode, no networking
3	Multi-user mode with networking	Starts the system
4	Not used/User-definable	For special purposes
5	Multi-user mode with GUI	Same as runlevel 3 with display manager
6	Reboot	Reboot the system

- Single-user mode
- Multi-user mode with no network services.
- Multi-user mode with network services.
- Shutdown
- Reboot

In modern GNU/Linux operating systems, System V runlevels have been deprecated. The common "init" process is systemd which has its own runlevels. While systemd is more powerful, it is more complex. As we are dealing with embedded systems, we do not need such a sophisticated init system as systemd. For this reason, we focus on the legacy Sysvinit package. With GNU/Linux systems, runlevels are assigned and used differently depending upon the distribution. Table 2.1 shows how runlevels for the Linux standard base (LSB). Display the current runlevel of the system with the command-line below:

```
$ who -r
          run-level 5  2017-08-23 17:42
```

2.4 The Root Filesystem

The GNU/Linux file space is organised into directories. The purpose of this directory structure is to impose some logical organisation on the filesystem. The files that support the operation of the system are stored within this file space:

- Kernel and loadable modules
- Second (and third) stage bootloaders
- Start-up/shutdown scripts
- Configuration files
- System utilities

The GNU/Linux file space may comprise several filesystems mounted at various points (directories) within the hierarchy. The root filesystem is mounted at the "/" directory (called the "root" directory) at the top of the hierarchy. Most of the files listed above are stored on the root filesystem but the kernel and bootloaders may be stored on another filesystem. GNU/Linux supports many different filesystem types, a few are listed below:

ext2/ext3/ext4:   The Extent filesystem is the default Linux filesystem. The original
     Extent filesystem, ext, has been deprecated and replaced with ext2, ext3 and ext4.
ReiserFS/Reiser4:   A journalling filesystem. Reiser4 is the successor to ReiserFS.
SquashFS: A read-only filesystem that compresses, files, directories and inodes.
     SquashFS is aimed at devices with limited storage, such as embedded systems.
XFS: A high performance journalling filesystem. Parallel I/O can be performed
     on XFS filesystems.
FAT/NTFS: Microsoft filesystems.
NFS: Network File System.

The command-line below shows the directory structure for an actual GNU/Linux system. For brevity we only show the hierarchy to a directory depth of two and omit any regular (or special) files:

```
# tree -dL 2 /
/
|-- bin
|-- boot
|   '-- extlinux
|-- dev
|   |-- misc
|   |-- shm
|   '-- ubd
|-- etc
|   |-- init.d
|   |-- network
|   |-- profile.d
|   |-- rc0.d
|   |-- rc1.d
|   |-- rc2.d
|   |-- rc3.d
|   |-- rc4.d
|   |-- rc5.d
|   |-- rc6.d
|   |-- rc.d
|   '-- rcS.d
|-- include
|   '-- ncurses
|-- lib
|   '-- modules
|-- proc
|-- root
```

```
|-- sbin
|-- share
|   |-- info
|   |-- locale
|   '-- man
|-- sys
|-- usr
|   |-- bin
|   |-- lib
|   |-- libexec
|   |-- sbin
|   '-- share
'-- var

39 directories
```

The GNU/Linux directory structure is defined in the filesystem hierarchy standard (FHS) and is governed by the Free Standards Group [2]. It is made up of a number of vendors, such as HP, Red Hat and IBM. The purpose of the FHS is to enable software and users to predict the location of files and directories. A description of some of the main directories is given below:

/bin: Essential command binaries. These are commands that can be used by all users, that is, administrators as well as regular users. The entries in the directory can either be hard links (binaries are actually in the directory) or symbolic links (binaries in some other directory). There must not be any subdirectories under /bin.

/boot: Bootloader files. The configuration files and further stages of the bootloader are kept under this directory, though they may be in subdirectories. The kernel file can also be in /boot (it could be in / instead).

/dev: Device and special files.

/etc: Host-specific system configuration files.

/lib: Shared libraries and kernel modules.

/media: Removable media mount point.

/mnt: Mount point for mounting a filesystem temporarily.

/opt: Add-on application software packages.

/sbin: Essential system binaries.

/srv: Data for services provided by this system

/tmp: Temporary files.

/usr: Secondary hierarchy.

/var: Contains variable data that changes frequently during the systems operation. For example, log files and caching data.

/root: Home directory for superuser.

/home: User home directories.

/proc: This is a virtual filesystem in which process and kernel information are kept. In the case of the GNU/Linux operating system, the filesystem, procfs is mounted here.

The filesystem will be discussed in greater detail in Chap. 4.

2.5 Process Management

Processes are programs under execution. The kernel is responsible for management and scheduling of processes on the system. Processes are created using the fork() system call. The fork() system call creates a replica of the process that made the call. Then one of the exec family of system calls is used to overlay the newly created process with a new program image. A detailed description of Unix/Linux system programming is outside the scope of this book. We refer the reader to [3] for a more detailed explanation. In this section we describe processes management.

2.5.1 Signals

Signals are software interrupts that notify processes that some condition or event has occurred, for example, divide by zero, illegal instruction executed or the Interrupt key is pressed. Furthermore, signals can be sent from other processes. Processes can respond to signals in three different ways:

- Perform the default action
- Ignore the signal
- Catch the signal and run a function

The default action performed by a process when it receives a signal depends on the signal type. Most (like SIGKILL) cause the process to terminate. Others like SIGQUIT cause the process to terminate and generate a core dump. A list of all the different signals can be displayed using the command:

```
$ kill -l
EXIT HUP INT QUIT ILL TRAP ABRT EMT FPE KILL BUS SEGV
SYS PIPE ALRM TERM USR1 USR2 CLD PWR WINCH URG POLL
STOP TSTP CONT TTIN TTOU VTALRM PROF XCPU XFSZ WAITING
LWP FREEZE THAW CANCEL LOST RTMIN RTMIN+1 RTMIN+2
RTMIN+3 RTMAX-3 RTMAX-2 RTMAX-1 RTMAX
```

Start a process to sleep for 300 s:

```
$ ( sleep 300 )
```

If we wish to terminate the process before five minutes has elapsed, we can send the process a signal. Some signals can be sent using keyboard control characters. The command below shows the mapping of control characters to signals for current terminal:

```
$ stty -a
speed 38400 baud; rows 40; columns 157; line = 0;
intr = ^C; quit = ^\; erase = ^?; kill = ^U; eof = ^D;
eol = M-^?; eol2 = M-^?; swtch = M-^?; start = ^Q;
stop = ^S; susp = ^Z; rprnt = ^R; werase = ^W;
lnext = ^V; flush = ^O; min = 1; time = 0;
-parenb -parodd cs8 hupcl -cstopb cread -clocal
-crtscts
-ignbrk brkint -ignpar -parmrk -inpck -istrip -inlcr
-igncr icrnl ixon -ixoff -iuclc ixany imaxbel iutf8
opost -olcuc -ocrnl onlcr -onocr -onlret -ofill -ofdel
nl0 cr0 tab0 bs0 vt0 ff0
isig icanon iexten echo echoe echok -echonl -noflsh
-xcase -tostop -echoprt echoctl echoke
```

We can see from the output above that the CONTROL-C key sequence generates an *intr* (SIGINT) signal. Press CONTROL-C to terminate the foreground process and return the shell prompt:

```
^C
$
```

If we run a process in background, we cannot send it signals using control characters from the keyboard. Instead we must use the kill command. To demonstrate, start another sleep process in background:

```
$ sleep 300 &
[1] 3603
```

The process id (PID), in this case, is 3603. We can confirm that the process is active:

```
$ ps -p 3603
  PID TTY          TIME CMD
 3603 pts/4    00:00:00 sleep
```

Send a SIGINT to the process 3603 with the kill command:

```
$ kill -SIGINT 3603
```

Now confirm process 3603 has terminated:

```
$ ps -p 3603
   PID TTY           TIME CMD
[1]+  Interrupt                 ( sleep 300 )
```

Traps are used to change the default behaviour of processes in response to signals. The command-line below starts a subshell. The trap statement changes the *disposition* of SIGINT. We do not specify an action so the disposition is to ignore the signal:

```
$ ( trap '' SIGINT ; sleep 300 ) &
[1] 3941
```

Confirm process 3941 is active:

```
$ ps -p 3941
   PID TTY         TIME CMD
  3941 pts/4    00:00:00 bash
```

Send a SIGINT to the process:

```
$ kill -SIGINT 3941
```

We see that process 3941 has ignored the signal:

```
$ ps -p 3941
   PID TTY         TIME CMD
  3941 pts/4    00:00:00 bash
```

We terminate the process with SIGTERM:

```
$ kill -SIGTERM 3941
$ ps -p 3941
   PID TTY           TIME CMD
[1]+  Terminated              ( trap '' SIGINT; sleep 300 )
```

If no signal is specified, the kill command sends SIGTERM (terminate signal) by default. Thus, the command-line above could have been replaced by `kill 3941`. Some signals cannot be ignored or caught. In the example below, we try to ignore SIGKILL:

```
$ ( trap '' SIGKILL ; sleep 300 ) &
[1] 3950
```

Regardless, the process terminates upon receiving SIGKILL:

```
$ kill -SIGKILL 3950
$ ps -p 3950
  PID TTY            TIME CMD
[1]+  Killed              ( trap '' SIGKILL; sleep 300 )
```

In this example we change the disposition to a specific action (note this time we run
the subshell in foreground):

```
$ ( trap 'echo "GOTCHA!"' INT ; sleep 300 )
```

Enter the CONTROL-C key sequence (generate SIGINT). On the SIGINT interrupt,
the signal handler invokes the signal's disposition action:

```
^CGOTCHA!
```

2.5.2 Job Control

If a program is run as a foreground process, it takes control of the terminal. Control
is returned to the shell when the foreground process terminates. Processes can be
started in the background (using the & operator), in which case, the shell retains
control of the terminal and the user can issue commands while the background
process runs. The process can be suspended using a SIGSTOP (or SIGTSTP) signal.
While this halts any further execution of the process, it does not terminate. Execution
of the process can be resumed from the point it initially suspended. Start a process
in foreground:

```
$ sleep 300 ; echo process ended
```

A SIGSTOP can be sent to the (foreground) process from the keyboard with a
CONTROL-Z:

```
^Z
[1]+  Stopped              sleep 300
```

The default disposition of SIGSTOP is to pause the foreground process. The command below shows the processes that are running and the states that they are in:

```
$ ps -o pid,ppid,state,wchan,comm
  PID  PPID S WCHAN  COMMAND
 4670  2155 S wait   bash
 5128  4670 T signal sleep
 5129  4670 R -      ps
```

Process 5129 is the process for the ps command that we issued above. It is in a
state running or runnable (R). Process 4670 is our shell process. It is in a state of

interruptable sleep due to the wait system call it issued after starting the ps command. The process we are interested in is 5128 which is the sleep 300 command we issued earlier and suspended with SIGSTOP. We can see it is in a state T which means stopped.

2.6 Process Input/Output

When a process is created, three I/O (input/output) streams are opened, namely, standard input, standard output and standard error. By default, standard input is mapped to the keyboard while standard output and standard error are mapped to the screen. The diagram in Fig. 2.1 shows a graphical representation of a processes (initial) I/O streams.

Table 2.2 shows a summary of the I/O streams. It shows that each I/O stream is associated with a *file descriptor*. When any file object is opened by a process, a file descriptor is created which is an index to the file object. Initially, file descriptors 0, 1 and 2 are mapped to devices, that is, keyboard (0) and screen (1 and 2). These file descriptors can be mapped to other file objects which can be other devices or regular files. This is called I/O *redirection*. The shell supports redirection of the standard I/O streams. In this section we present a number of examples of I/O redirection.

The > operator is used to redirect standard output. We use the date command to demonstrate. The function of the date command is to display the current time and

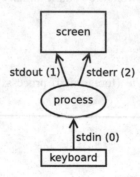

Fig. 2.1 Process Input/output

Table 2.2 Summary of input/output streams

File descriptor	Stream name	Abbreviation	Default device
0	Standard input	stdin	Keyboard
1	Standard output	stdout	Screen
2	Standard error	stderr	Screen

date on stdout. Without specifying any redirection, the time and date is displayed on the screen:

```
$ date
Mon Sep 16 15:29:15 BST 2013
```

We run the command again but this time we redirect stdout to a file *datefile*:

```
$ date > datefile
```

We see nothing displayed on the screen. If we examine *datefile*, we see that it contains the time and date of when the date command was run:

```
$ cat datefile
Mon Sep 16 15:32:05 BST 2013
```

As *datefile* did not exist before we issued the date command, the stdout redirection operator caused the shell to create it. If *datefile* had already existed, its content would have been overwritten by the output of date. The » operator also redirects stdout to a file, but unlike > it appends the output of a command to the current content. For example:

```
$ date >> datefile
$ cat datefile
Mon Sep 16 15:32:14 BST 2013
Mon Sep 16 15:32:34 BST 2013
```

The < operator redirects a file to stdin of a process. In the example we use the dc command which is a calculator that accepts mathematical expressions in reverse-polish notation. By default, dc reads stdin (in this case is the keyboard) for instructions. We enter the string "2 3 + p" and process outputs the answer (5):

```
$ dc
2 3 + p
5
```

To show how stdin can be redirected from a file, create a file with an expression in reverse polish notation:

```
$ echo "2 3 + p" > dcfile
```

Now run dc and redirect *dcfile* to stdin:

```
$ dc < dcfile
5
```

Standard input can also be redirected from Here documents using the « operator. A Here document is a literal input stream that appears within the source code itself. In the example below, EOF is used as a delimiter to indicate the beginning and end of the contents of the Here document:

```
$ dc <<-EOF
> 2 3 + p
> 10 * p
> EOF
5
50
```

Standard output and standard error are separate streams even though they both default to the screen. As they are separate streams, they can be redirected separately. Consider the command-line below:

```
$ time date
Tue Sep 17 11:14:35 BST 2013

real    0m0.004s
user    0m0.004s
sys     0m0.004s
```

As we know, the date command displays the current time and date. The time command displays the system resources that the date command used (in terms of real, user and system time). If we repeat the command, but this time redirect stdout, we see that the output of the date command has been redirected to *datefile* but the output from the time command still appears on the screen. This is because the output of the time command is on stderr.

```
$ time date > datefile

real    0m0.005s
user    0m0.004s
sys     0m0.004s
$ cat datefile
Tue Sep 17 11:32:22 BST 2013
```

We can redirect stderr with the 2> operator:

```
$ (time date) 2> timefile
Tue Sep 17 11:37:32 BST 2013
$ cat timefile

real    0m0.004s
user    0m0.004s
sys     0m0.004s
```

We can see that the output of the time command (stderr) is redirected to *timefile*. The output of the date command (stdout) is unaffected and is displayed on the screen.

Both stdout and stderr can be redirected to a single file by combining both streams with the 2 > &1 operator and redirecting stdout to *tdfile*:

```
$ (time date) > tdfile 2>&1
$ cat tdfile
Tue Sep 17 11:40:16 BST 2013

real    0m0.004s
user    0m0.000s
sys     0m0.008s
```

It is also possible to redirect the standard output of one process to standard input of another. The | operator is called a *pipe*. Pipes are a Unix interprocess communication (IPC) mechanism [3]. The example below generates a DNS request for the NS records of the ac.uk domain. The output of the command produces a number of lines of output. We filter out all but the actual NS records by piping the output of dig to the grep command:

```
$ dig ac.uk NS | grep "^ac"
ac.uk.    60177   IN      NS      ns2.ja.net.
ac.uk.    60177   IN      NS      ns0.ja.net.
ac.uk.    60177   IN      NS      ns1.surfnet.nl.
ac.uk.    6017    IN      NS      ws-fra1.win-ip.dfn.de.
ac.uk     6017    IN      NS      ns3.ja.net.
ac.uk     60177   IN      NS      ns4.ja.net.
ac.uk     60177   IN      NS      auth03.ns.uu.net.
```

A summary of redirection operators are shown in Table 2.3.

Table 2.3 Redirection operators

Operator	Action
<	Redirect stdin
>	Redirect stdout
»	Append to stdout
«	Redirect from here document
2>	Redirect stderr
2 > &1	Redirect stderr to stdout
|	Pipe stdout to stdin of another process
2 > &1 |	Pipe stdout and stderr to stdin of another process

2.7 The Process Environment

Every process has an *environment*. The environment of a process is a NULL terminated character array list. Each element in the list is an environment variable of the
form *name = value*. Environment variables can be created, deleted and set during
the execution period of the process. This section describes the Unix process environment and the system call functions available for accessing it. The C program in
Listing 2.1 declares a pointer to a character array, *env*. Each element of the array is
displayed to the screen.

Listing 2.1 *Contents of shenv.c*

```
#include <stdio.h>

main(int argc, char **argv, char **env)
{
    while(*env != (char *) 0)
        printf("%s\n", *env++);
}
```

Compile *shenv.c* and execute it. The program will output many lines. For brevity, we
pipe it through a filter so that only the value of the SHELL variable is displayed:

```
$ gcc -o shenv shenv.c
$ ./shenv | grep SHELL
/bin/bash
```

The environment of a process can also be accessed using the global *environ* variable.
The code extract below demonstrates its use:

```
char **p=environ;
while(*p != (char *) 0)
    printf("%s\n", *p++);
```

The value of individual environment variables can be accessed using the
getenv() function. Create a file *get_env.c* with the contents shown in Listing 2.2.

Listing 2.2 *Contents of getenv.c*

```
/* get environment variables */
#include <stdlib.h>
main(int argc, char **argv, char **env)
{
    int ret;
    char *value;

    if(argc<2)
```

```
      {
            printf("usage: %s name\n", argv[0]);
            exit(-1);
      }

      if((env_val=getenv(argv[1])) < 0)
            printf("error running getenv\n");
      printf("%s\n", value);
}
```

Compile *getenv.c* then execute the resultant binary code with a variable name as an argument:

```
$ ./getenv SHELL
/bin/bash
```

Environment variables can be set with the setenv() function. Listing 2.3 shows the program for setting an environment variable. Compile it in the usual way.

Listing 2.3 *Contents of setenv.c*

```
/* set environment variables */
#include <stdlib.h>
main(int argc, char **argv, char **env)
{
      int ret;
      char *value;

      if(argc<3)
      {
            printf("usage: %s name value [0|1]\n", argv[0]);
            exit(-1);
      }

      value=getenv(argv[1]);
      printf("value of %s before setenv() is %s\n", argv[1], value);
      if(setenv(argv[1], argv[2], atoi(argv[3]))<0)
            printf("error with setenv function\n");

      value=getenv(argv[1]);
      printf("value of %s after setenv() is %s\n", argv[1], value);
}
```

Execute setenv with three arguments, that is: a variable name, the value to set the variable to and an overwrite parameter. If an existing variable is specified then it

will only change to the specified value if the overwrite is 1. In the example below
the variable GREET already exists. The value of GREET is unchanged after the
setenv() function call because the overwrite parameter is 0.

```
$ ./setenv GREET hello
GREET before setenv() is (null)
GREET after setenv() is hello
```

Set the GREET variable from the command-line:

```
$ export GREET="welcome"
```

An attempt to set GREET fails because the overwrite flag is 0 (by default):

```
./setenv GREET hello
GREET before setenv() is welcome
GREET after setenv() is welcome
```

Setting the overwrite flag explicitly to a non-zero value sets the environment variable:

```
$ ./setenv GREET hello 1
GREET before setenv() is welcome
GREET after setenv() is hello
```

Environment variables can also be created and set with the function putenv(). The
putenv() function places an entry onto the environment list in the form name=value.
If the variable does not exist then it is created. If it does exist, the old entry is replaced.
Create a file *putenv.c* with the contents shown in Listing 2.4.

Listing 2.4 *Contents of putenv.c*

```
/* put environment variables */
#include <stdlib.h>

main(int argc, char **argv, char **env)
{
    int ret, i=0;
    char *value, name[32], *p;
    if(argc<2)
    {
        perror("usage: %s name value [0|1]\n", argv[0]);
        exit(1);
    }

    for(p=argv[1]; *p != '='; p++, i++)
        name[i]=*p;
    name[i]=(char) 0;
```

```
    env_val=getenv(env_name);
    printf("value of %s before putenv() is %s\n", name, value);

    if(putenv(argv[1]) != 0)
        perror("error with putenv function\n");

    value=getenv(name);
    printf("value of %s after putenv() is %s\n", name, value);

}
```

Compile *putenv.c* then execute the binary code:

```
$ putenv GREET=welcome
value of GREET before putenv() is hello world
value of GREET after putenv() is welcome
```

Child processes do not inherit environment variables unless they are *exported*. Run shenv and pipe through a filter.

```
$ ./shenv | grep GREET
```

The execution of the command-line above results in no output. This is because the variable GREET has not been exported in the shell and is not inherited by the child process (in this case shenv). Export the variable GREET:

```
$ export greeting
$ ./shenv | grep GREET
GREET=hello
```

2.7.1   Shell Parameters

The shell, like any other Unix process has an environment. The shell's environment can be accessed through its parameters from the command-line. There are three types of parameter:

- named parameters
- positional parameters
- special parameters

Named parameters are known as environment variables. Some of these variables are initialised when the user logs in. The shell uses these variables to determine its behaviour. The shell also maintains certain variables throughout the login session, some of which are defined by the shell and are given special meaning, while others can be user defined.

Positional parameters enable reference to arguments supplied to shell scripts. The shell shares process information through special parameters. Special parameters can be accessed by the user, but unlike named and positional parameters, they can only be set by the shell itself.

Named parameters are assigned using the command line statement in the form name=value. Variable names are alphanumeric strings, they can contain numeric characters or underscores but must begin with an alphabetic character. Five examples are presented below:

```
$ n=2
$ n2=4
$ N=3
$ MYNAME=alan
$ greeting="hello world"
```

Note that Unix is case sensitive, so the variable "name" is not the same as "Name". A variable can be expanded (evaluated) by preceding the variable name with a $, for example:

```
$ echo $greeting
hello world
```

Variables can be concatenated:

```
$ day=21 month=01 year=2006
$ echo $day$month$year
21012006
```

One needs to take care when concatenating literals with variables. The example below uses variables for the day and month but hard-codes the year:

```
$ echo $day$month2006
05
```

The problem is that the shell cannot distinguish between the variable name month and the literal value 2006. It, therefore, tries to expand a variable with the variable name month2006, which is not set. This can be rectified by surrounding the variables names with braces { }, for example:

```
$ echo ${day}${month}2006
05112006
```

Although the braces are not always necessary, it is good practice to use them when evaluating variables.

2.7.2 Quoting

Consider the following example, where the variable expansion phrase is enclosed in double quotes:

```
$ echo "echo $greeting", displays $greeting
echo hello world, displays hello world
```

Variables enclosed in double quotes are still expanded by the shell. To prevent expansion, variables should be enclosed in single quotes. To display the string "echo $greeting" verbatim, use the statement:

```
$ echo 'echo $greeting', displays $greeting
echo $greeting, displays hello world
```

2.7.3 Positional Parameters

Positional parameters provide a means of accessing arguments to shell scripts. They are referenced by the numbers 1, 2, 3,... etc, where the numbers reflect the order in which the arguments appeared on the command-line (from left to right). Positional parameters cannot be assigned in the same way as named parameters. For example you cannot do this:

```
$ 1=hello
1=hello: command not found
```

Positional parameters are assigned when a shell script is invoked with command-line arguments but they can be assigned with the set command:

```
$ set 'uptime'
```

This causes the space separated strings from the output of uptime to be assigned to the positional parameters. The statement below shows the values of all positional parameters that were assigned:

```
$ echo $*
Linux underworld 2.6.32-26-generic-pae #48-Ubuntu SMP
Wed Nov 24 10:31:20 UTC 2010 i686 GNU/Linux
```

The command-line below gives the number of assigned positional parameters (equivalent to argc in C):

```
$ echo $#
13
```

If we specifically want the kernel version, then we evaluate the third positional parameter:

```
$ echo $3
2.6.32-26-generic-pae
```

Double digit positional parameters need to be enclosed in braces:

```
$ echo ${12}
i686
```

Finally, positional parameter 0 is set to the name of the current process (equivalent to `argv[0]` in C), which in this case should be the name of the shell command itself:

```
$ echo $0
bash
```

2.7.4 Special Parameters

Special parameters can be accessed by the user but can only be assigned (directly) by the shell, typically in response to some event. We have already encountered the $*$ and # parameters which are set when a command is invoked with arguments (or with the set command).

The ? parameter expands to the return code of the process that last exited. If we enclose a command line statement in brackets it is executed in a subshell. The command-line below starts a new shell and immediately issues exit. The argument following exit is the value of the subshell's return code (255 in this case):

```
$ (exit 255)
```

The return code of the child process can be accessed by the parent through the ? parameter. If a process terminated normally then the return code is likely to be zero. If the process terminated due to some error condition, it should set a non-zero return code so that the parent can determine the reason for the termination:

```
$ echo $?
255
```

The process ID of the shell is stored in the $ parameter. The ps command shows that the process ID of the foreground shell is 10005, which is what is given by the expansion of $:

```
$ ps | grep bash
10005 pts/77              00:00:00 bash
$ echo $$
10005
```

The ! parameter evaluates to the process ID of the last background process. To demonstrate, the statement below invokes the sleep command (which sleeps for 60 s) in the background:

```
$ sleep 60 &
[1] 24835
```

The process ID of the background process is displayed on the screen (in this case 24835). Expansion of the ! parameter confirms this:

```
$ echo $!
24835
```

As we saw in the section above, processes do not inherit environment variables from their parent unless the variables are exported. Here, we explore shell variable exportation further. The command-line below displays the process ID of the current process followed by the value of greeting (which was assigned earlier):

```
$ echo ${greeting?parameter not set}
hello world
```

If we start a new shell and issue the command again we see that greeting is not set in the child process:

```
$ bash
$ echo ${greeting?parameter not set}
bash: greeting: parameter not set
```

Terminate the current shell process and return to the parent, then export greeting:

```
$ exit
$ export greeting
```

Confirm that a variable has the export attribute set by typing:

```
$ export | grep greeting
declare -x greeting="hello world"
```

Now start a new shell again and evaluate greeting:

```
$ bash
$ echo ${greeting?parameter not set}
hello world
```

The new shell has inherited the variable greeting. A variable retains its export attribute
(until the shell is terminated) even if it is reassigned, but it can be removed using the
typeset command:

```
$ typeset +x greeting
$ export | grep greeting       # yields no result
```

In Bash (but not the original Bourne shell), a variable can be assigned and exported
in one command-line statement:

```
$ export greeting="hi there"
$ export | grep greeting
declare -x greeting="hi there"
```

2.8 Virtual Machines

One of the problems of the previous edition of this book is that it required the reader
to replicate the authors' environment in order to successfully build the software in
the worked examples. At the time of the release of the first edition, replicating the
authors environment may have been inconvenient. Several years on, replicating that
environment is problematic as versions of utilities and libraries have moved on. Not
only that but most commercially available PCs are 64-bit, whereas we still need to
build software for a 32-bit target. Even though both host and target are Intel based
machines the difference in word length means we would, effectively, need to cross
compile. We resolve the "cross-compilation" problem by using a 32-bit virtual
machine.

This section describes virtualisation methods in general but also covers how to
install and configure the virtual machine technologies that we will use in later chapters
where we use them to build actual GNU/Linux operating systems.

We also use a *container* technology called Docker. While containers are not actual
virtual machines, they do offer a useful level of virtualisation that isolates processes
from the host system. We also use these methods to test the system at various stages
of the build rather than leaving it to the point at which it is bootstrapped on the actual
hardware. Containers will be discussed in more detail in Chap. 3.

Operating systems provide a layer of abstraction above the computer system's hardware. The operating system virtualises many of the physical resources of a computer, for example:

- Memory.
- Disks and disk partitions
- Network interfaces and bridges

Modern computers are sufficiently powerful to use virtualisation to present the illusion of many virtual machines, each running a separate instance of the operating system. Virtualisation is not a new concept (virtual memory, for example, was conceived in the 1950s). IBM introduced the VM/370 operating system for its 370 architecture mainframes in the 1960s. The VM/370 environment comprises two software components, namely, the control program (CP) and the conversational monitor system (CMS). CP performs resource management and creates the virtual machine environment in which an operating system can run (see Fig. 2.2).

CMS is an interactive development environment. It runs as a guest in a CP virtual machine. CMS provides program development and personal computing functions in an interactive fashion to an individual terminal user. That is, CMS gives each user the illusion they are the sole user of a VM/370 operating system. While each CMS user uses a separate virtual machine, the code is shared between them. Other operating systems, such as DOS/VS, MVS, OS/MFT, OS/MVT and SVS can also run under CP. CP can even run in a virtual machine under the control of CP itself.

Guest operating systems run under the control of a hypervisor. There are two classifications of hypervisors, namely Type 1 and Type 2. Type 1 hypervisors run natively on the host's hardware. Type 2 hypervisors are *hosted*, that is, they run on a host operating system. The diagram in Fig. 2.3 illustrates the difference between the two hypervisor types. Below, we describe a number of virtualisation technologies:

Quick emulator (Qemu):   Qemu is a hosted hypervisor virtualisation technology. Qemu supports a number of operating systems, including GNU/Linux, BSD, Solaris and Microsoft Windows. It also supports a number of architectures, namely, x86, ARM, MIPS, PowerPC and SPARC (amongst others).

Bochs: Bochs is an emulator for PC compatible hardware. It is distributed under the GNU Lesser General Public License (GLPL).

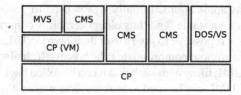

Fig. 2.2 VM/370 architecture

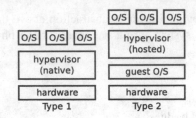

Fig. 2.3 Type 1 and Type 2 hypervisors

VMware: VMware is a company that specialises in virtualisation technology. They offer both type 1 (ESX Server) and type 2 (VMware Workstation and VMware Player) hypervisor products.

User mode Linux (UML):   User mode Linux (UML) is a Linux kernel compiled as a regular ELF file so that it can be run as a user process.

VirtualBox: VirtualBox is an open-source hypervisor originally developed by Sun Microsystems. It is currently developed by Oracle as Sun Microsystems was bought by Oracle in 2010. VirtualBox runs on a number of host operating systems, including: Solaris, GNU/Linux, macOS, Windows and FreeBSD.

VirtualBox adopts a standard software-based virtualisation approach which supports 32-bit guest OSs. We make use of this feature as we need to compile software for 32-bit Intel processors. As most commodity computer systems are now 64-bit, it obviates the need to cross-compile. In this book we use Vagrant as an *orchestration* tool for running VirtualBox virtual machines.

The following two subsections discuss two virtual machine technologies from the list above, namely, UML and VirtualBox. We use these two technolgoies in this book to build and test the software we build. We also use the Docker container system which will be discussed later. With VirtualBox, we also introduce Vagrant which is a provisioning tool and is useful for setting up virtual machines.

2.8.1   User Mode Linux

User Mode Linux (UML) is a modification of the Linux kernel so that it can run as a guest on top of a host's kernel. A UML kernel is executed as a regular user process and no hardware virtualisation is necessary. Figure 2.4 shows the UML architecture.

UML has numerous applications. Initially it was used to test "bleeding edge" kernels on a host running a stable (and thus older) kernel. A common application is teaching and research. It is possible to give a user their own GNU/Linux environment in which to experiment without compromising the host itself. It also makes it easy to take snapshots of the UML filesystem such that it can be rolled back in the event of an unrecoverable failure. UML can be used to host services within its own environment

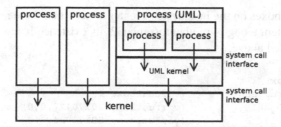

Fig. 2.4 User mode Linux

thereby providing some separation from the host system. Docker, however, mostly fulfils this requirement now (see below). We use UML as a tool for testing the embedded operating systems built in this book. The UML feature is part of the Linux kernel and is invoked when the kernel is configured and compiled.

2.8.2 VirtualBox and Vagrant

As mentioned above, VirtualBox is an open-source hypervisor for running virtual machines. VirtualBox can be installed with the package management system, thus:

```
$ sudo apt-get install virtualbox
```

Vagrant is a tool for building and managing virtual machine environments. Vagrant was originally developed for VirtualBox, however, support has been added for Hyper-V, Docker, VMware, and AWS. Nevertheless, we confine our discussion to configuration and provision of VirtualBox virtual machines. Vagrant (and associated packages) can be installed with the package manager:

```
$ sudo apt-get install vagrant \
> golang-github-hashicorp-atlas-go-dev
```

The foundation of Vagrant is the *box* which is a packaged environment. Typically, this is a virtual machine with some pre-configured software (operating system, utilities, libraries etc). Note that, Vagrant now supports Docker, in which case, a box could be a container (see subsection below). As we are using Vagrant to provision VirtualBox, we are only concerned with virtual machine boxes here. Boxes can be built from scratch but there are many "third party" boxes available on which to base a virtual machine. As an example, add an Ubuntu 16.04 LTS box to your host machine:

```
$ vagrant box add ubuntu/xenial64
```

List the Vagrant boxes on the host system. It can be seen that there are a number of boxes on the system along with ubuntu/xenial32, its existence being a result of the command executed above:

```
$ vagrant box list
hashicorp/precise64        (virtualbox, 1.1.0)
ubuntu/precise64           (virtualbox, 20170427.0.0)
ubuntu/xenial64       .    (virtualbox, 20170724.0.0)
```

The file *Vagrantfile* contains the specification for the type of virtual machine and how it is configured and provisioned. The statements in the Vagrantfile are Ruby statements. Create a Vagrantfile:

```
$ vagrant init
A 'Vagrantfile' has been placed in this directory. You
are now ready to 'vagrant up' your first virtual
environment! Please read the comments in the Vagrantfile
as well as documentation on 'vagrantup.com' for more
information on using Vagrant.
```

The Vagrantfile contains many file lines, but most are commented out. The contents of the Vagrantfile, with the comment lines omitted, looks like this:

```
Vagrant.configure(2) do |config|

  config.vm.box = "base"

end
```

Edit Vagrantfile so that the line `config.vm.box = "base"` reads:

```
  config.vm.box = "ubuntu/xenial64"
```

Run the virtual machine:

```
$ vagrant up
```

SSH into the virtual machine:

```
$ vagrant ssh
Welcome to Ubuntu 16.04.2 LTS (GNU/Linux 4.4.0-87-generic i686)

  * Documentation:  https://help.ubuntu.com
  * Management:     https://landscape.canonical.com
  * Support:        https://ubuntu.com/advantage
```

```
    Get cloud support with Ubuntu Advantage Cloud Guest:
       http://www.ubuntu.com/business/services/cloud

0 packages can be updated.
0 updates are security updates.


Last login: Wed Jul 26 13:22:48 2017 from 10.0.2.2
ubuntu@ubuntu-xenial:~$
```

Check the Linux kernel version:

```
ubuntu@ubuntu-xenial:~$ uname -nor
ubuntu-xenial 4.4.0-87-generic GNU/Linux
```

Exit from the virtual machine and drop back to the host:

```
ubuntu@ubuntu-xenial:~$ exit
logout
Connection to 127.0.0.1 closed.
$
```

Halt the virtual machine:

```
$ vagrant halt
```

2.9 Summary

In this chapter we discussed the component parts a GNU/Linux system, namely the bootloader, kernel and filesystem. In later chapters we will describe, in detail, how to build these components.

Once the system has booted (init process has been initialised), system daemons and user applications are run as processes, where processes are programs under execution. Processes are managed by the kernel. We covered process management (signals and job control), input/output and the process environment.

References

1. Linux Kernel Organization, Inc. The Linux Kernel Archives, https://www.kernel.org/. Accessed 22 Jul 2013

2. Filesystem Hierarchy Standard Group, http://refspecs.linuxfoundation.org/FHS_2.3/fhs-2.3. pdf. Accessed 24 Jul 2013
3. K. Haviland, B. Salama, *Unix System Programming* (Addison-Weseley, Boston, USA, 1987)

Containers

3

Containers are a form of operating system virtualisation but, unlike virtual machines, they do not virtualise the underlying hardware and are, therefore, less resource intensive than a full virtual machine.

Deploying an application on diverse systems can be problematic due to the application's *dependencies*. The dependency tree for an application can be quite complex as even the application's immediate dependencies have dependencies themselves. Sophisticated package management systems, such Apt, resolve many of these dependency problems. However, for developers sharing source code (say, through git repositories) the environment set up by the package management system may not be sufficient. Developers may need *bleeding edge* versions of software libraries or even versions that are older than the *stable* versions on the host system. If they are working on embedded systems, then they may need stripped down versions of the libraries that exist on their desktop host.

Package management systems continually upgrade software on the host (to fix bugs and implement security patches) and at some point it may be necessary to upgrade the entire distribution as support for it will eventually come to an end. Therefore, any computer platform is rarely quiescent in terms of the versions of its software. A piece of software that could be successfully compiled one day may not successfully compile the next. Furthermore, a piece of software that compiles on one developer's machine may not compile on another's. It is important to keep the development environment as stable and reliable as possible. Added to this, in a distributed development environment, it needs to be consistent across developers' machines.

Containers facilitate the development, shipment and execution of applications. Applications are wrapped in a container along with utilities and the shared-libraries upon which they depend, thereby solving the *works-on my machine* problem. The literature goes to great lengths to emphasise that containers are *not* virtual machines. Indeed, for a given host, any application running within a Docker container still

© Springer International Publishing AG, part of Springer Nature 2018   41
A. Holt and C.-Y. Huang, *Embedded Operating Systems*, Undergraduate
Topics in Computer Science, https://doi.org/10.1007/978-3-319-72977-0_3

uses the same kernel as an application running natively on that host. In contrast, an application running on a virtual machine runs on a separate (and probably different) kernel to that of the host. The main benefit as far as this book is concerned is that it ensures a common environment across reader/author hosts. Build environments can be precisely specified and carefully controlled so that they do not affect the host machine and vice-versa.

A popular container technology is Docker [1–3]. Docker is not the only Linux container system but it is the one we use in this book. In Sect. 3.2 we describe how to install Docker and give examples of how it can be used. In later chapters we use Docker to build various components of operating systems.

The Linux kernel supports a number of isolation features, namely, namespaces and control groups (cgroups). Namespace are an abstraction of some system-wide resource. A process running in a specific namespace appears to have its own instance of a resource, thereby isolating it from the rest of the system. We describe namespaces in the section below.

Cgroups are a means of limiting the system resources processes (or process groups) can consume. A detailed explanation of cgroups is beyond the scope of this book.

3.1   Linux Namespaces

Namespaces (along with cgroups) is one of the main kernel technologies that facilitates containers. A process that exists within a particular namespace has a restricted view of some aspect of the system. The category of Linux namespace types is provided in the list below. Processes that exist within the *root* namespace have a system-wide view of the host's resources.

Mount: Isolates a process from mounted filesystems. The mount namespace is the set of mount filesystems that a process can see. This set may be different from a process running natively on the host or a process running in another namespace (which has its own mounted filesystem set). A process within a mount namespace can change its set of mount filesystems (mount new ones or unmount exiting ones) without affecting processes running outside of the namespace.

UTS: Isolates the hostname and the domain names. The hostname in a namespace can be changed without affecting the hostname of the host itself.

IPC: Isolates certain interprocess communication (IPC) resources, namely, POSIX message queues and System V IPC mechanisms.

PID: Isolates the process ID number space. Processes in different namespaces (including the host), therefore, may have the same process ID value. Note that, a process running in a namespace will have two process IDs. One ID in the namespace itself and one in the host system. The values of the two process IDs need not be the same (except by random chance).

Network: Isolates system network resources. Each namespace has its own network devices, IP addresses, TCP/UDP ports and routing tables.

User: Isolates users and groups. User and group IDs in a namespace are different from those on the host system (or any other namespace). The benefit of this is that a process could be given privileged (superuser) access to resources within the user namespace while access to resources outside are unprivileged.

Unix systems have long had an *isolation* feature in the chroot system call. The chroot system call changes a process's *perception* of its / (root) directory. A subdirectory under the filesystem hierarchy can be specified as a processes new "/" directory. While chroot is not a kernel namespace, it can provide rudimentary containment for a process.

We demonstrate namespaces by writing a utility to run a process in a *contained* environment. Accompanying this book is a git repository with some useful files. One of the files is a tarball of a simple GNU/Linux root file structure. Use git clone to fetch the repository for this book:

```
$ mkdir ~/emxlbook && cd ~/emxbook
$ git clone https://github.com/agholt/emx.git
```

In the directory *emx/chapter3* is the root file structure tarball, untar it with the command-line below:

```
$ tar zxf emx/chapter3/emx.tar.gz
```

This creates a directory called *root* in the current working directory (which should be in *~/emxbook*). The directory, *root*, contains a root directory structure for a GNU/Linux system, in fact it is the directory structure that we will build later in Chap. 6. It contains all the administration files, shared libraries, start up scripts, utilities and device files necessary for a GNU/Linux operating system. The only component that it is missing is a Linux kernel but we do not need one at this stage because a container system uses the host's kernel. Examine the contents of the directory, *root*:

```
$ ls root/
bin     dev     lib       proc    sbin    usr     var.tar
boot    etc     linuxrc   root    sys     var
```

Run the chroot command on the directory, *root*. This drops us into a chroot *jail* and runs a shell process:

```
$ sudo chroot root /bin/sh -i
/ #
```

The prompt tell us that we are in a directory with the pathname of /. We can check this explicitly with the pwd command:

```
/ # pwd
/
```

While our directory pathname is given as /, we are actually in the *~/emxbook/root*. The directory *~/emxbook/root* on the host is the same as the / in the chroot jail. We can confirm this by viewing the contents of the directory:

```
/ # ls
bin     dev     lib       proc    sbin    usr     var.tar
boot    etc     linuxrc   root    sys     var
```

We can see the contents is same as the *~/emxbook/root* directory (shown above). Note that, the commands we are running (sh, ls, pwd etc) and their shared libraries exist within this directory structure. In the chroot jail, the system-wide utilities (and shared libraries) are unavailable to us. We present one last demonstration of the change of root by listing the inode number of the "." and ".." directories:

```
/ # ls -di . ..
10240432 .  10240432 ..
```

Recall that, "." is a reference to the current directory and ".." to the parent directory. The ls commands yields the same inode number for both. The / directory is the only directory where both "." and ".." point to the same directory. Although there *is* a directory on the host system above /, we are *contained* within the chroot jail and cannot access any directories outside of it (that is, until we exit from the current shell process). Exit from the container and change directory to *root*. Check the inode number of the "." and ".." directories. We see that the inode number of "." is the same as / in the chroot jail. However, the inode number of ".." is different from "." because the parent directory is accessible:

```
/ # exit
$ cd root/
$ ls -di . ..
10240432 .  10240435 ..
```

3.1.1   Using Namespaces to Build a Container

In this subsection we develop our own, albeit rudimentary, container system using namespaces. We demonstrate container technology using just two of the namespace abstractions, namely, the PID namespace and the UTS namespace. For convenience we use chroot for filesystem isolation. The C code for container_demo is given in Listing 3.1. Most of the code is concerned with processing the command-line options and arguments. The usage message for the program is given below:

```
container_demo [-pu] <root_dir> [program]
```

The options -p and -u specify that the process should be placed in the PID and UTS namespace, respectively (these are the only namespaces the utility support, but it is sufficient for demonstration purposes). The <root_dir> is a mandatory argument and specifies the chroot directory. For simplicity, we use chroot to isolate the process rather than the mount namespace. The optional argument specifies which program to execute in the namespace(s). If the argument is omitted, then the default program is */bin/sh*. Once the options and arguments are processed, the container() function is called:

```
container(flags,root_dir);
```

The flags argument reflect the namespaces in which the process runs and we can control them with command-line options. The -p option adds CLONE_NEWPID to the flags variable and the -u option adds CLONE_NEWUTS:

```
case 'p':  // PID Namespace
    flags |= CLONE_NEWPID;
    :
  case 'u': // UTS Namespace
    flags |= CLONE_NEWUTS;
    :
```

Obviously, if either of the options are not used, the respective namespaces are not applied. The root_dir argument specifies the chroot directory. The next process created is placed in the namespaces indicated by the flags passed to container(). That process is created by the run_proc() function which takes one argument, namely, the pathname of the program that runs in the process:

```
run_proc(p);
```

By default, this is */bin/sh*, but it can be overridden with a command-line argument.

Listing 3.1 *Contents of* container_demo.c

```
#define _GNU_SOURCE
#include <stdio.h>
#include <stdlib.h>
#include <string.h>
#include <unistd.h>
#include <sched.h>
```

```
extern int container(int, char *);
extern int run_proc(char *);

int main (int argc, char **argv) {

    int c;
    char *root_dir, *p = "/bin/sh";
    int flags = 0;

    char usage_msg[64];
    snprintf(usage_msg, sizeof usage_msg, \
            "USAGE: %s [-pu] <chroot_dir>\n", argv[0]);


    // process options and set namespace flags
    while ((c = getopt (argc, argv, "pu")) != -1)
        switch (c)
        {
            case 'p':  // PID Namespace
                flags |= CLONE_NEWPID;
                break;
            case 'u': // UTS Namespace
                flags |= CLONE_NEWUTS;
                break;
            case '?':
                fprintf (stderr, \
                    "Unknown option '-%c'.\n", optopt);
                return 1;
            default:
                abort ();
        }

    // chroot directory is a mandatory arg
    if (argv[optind] == NULL) {
        fprintf(stderr, "%s", usage_msg);
        exit(1);
    }

    root_dir = argv[optind];
    if (argv[optind+1] != NULL)
        p = argv[optind+1];

    // contain process
    if(container(flags,root_dir) == -1)
        exit(1);
```

```
        run_proc(p); // run process in new container

}
```

Listing 3.2 shows the source code for the function, container(). The unshare() system call sets the namespaces. These settings take effect on the next process that is created. Once the namespaces are set up (according to the value of flags) chroot() and chdir() system calls are issued to change the processes root and working directory.

Listing 3.2 *Contents of* container.c

```
#define _GNU_SOURCE
#include <stdio.h>
#include <unistd.h>
#include <sched.h>

int container(int flags, char *root_dir) {

    // set namespaces
    if (unshare(flags) == -1) {
        printf("unshare failed\n");
        return -1;
    }

    //change root and cd to "/"
    if(chroot(root_dir) == -1)  {
        printf("chroot failed\n");
        return -1;
    }

    if(chdir("/") == -1)   {
        printf("chdir failed\n");
    }

    return 0;
}
```

The source code for *run_proc.c* is shown in Listing 3.3. The run_proc() function creates the new process using the fork() and execl() system calls. The fork() system creates a new process by generating a replica of itself. The parent process (that called the fork() issues a wait() system call and sleeps on the exit event of the child process). The child process (which resulted from the fork()) issues a execl() system call. This replaces the current process image with a new process image.

Listing 3.3 *Contents of* run_proc.c

```
#define _GNU_SOURCE
#include <stdio.h>
#include <unistd.h>
#include <sys/wait.h>
#include <sys/mount.h>
#include <libgen.h>

extern int container(int, char *);

int run_proc(char *p) {

    int pid, status;
    char *n;


    pid = fork();

    switch(pid)
    {
        case 0:

            // mount procfs
            if(mount("proc", "/proc", \
                            "proc", 0, "") == -1) {
                printf("procfs mount failed\n");
                return -1;
            }

            sethostname("emx", 3); // set hostname

            n = basename(p);
            execl(p, n, (char *)0); // exec process, p
            break;

        case -1:
            printf ("fork failed\n");
            break;

        default:
            wait(&status);
            if (umount("/proc") == -1)
                printf("umount failed\n");
            break;
```

```
        } // switch case closed

        return(0);


}
```

We need to compile the source files above into an executable binary file. In order
to simplify the compilation process, we use the make utility. Create a file called
Makefile with the contents shown in Listing 3.4.

Listing 3.4 *Contents of* Makefile

```
OBJECTS = container_demo.o run_sh.o container.o

default:     container_demo

%.o:         %.c
             gcc -c $< -o $@

container_demo: $(OBJECTS)
             gcc $(OBJECTS) -o $@

clean:
             -rm -f $(OBJECTS)
             -rm -f container_demo
```

Compile the container_demo utility:

```
$ make
```

3.1.2 Demonstrate the Container

First we will demonstrate how the UTS namespace works. In a UTS namespace the
hostname can be different from the hostname in the root namespace. Just before the
container_demo program execs, it sets the hostname in the container (to "emx").
We verify the hostname of the host system (root namespace) before we invoke con-
tainer_demo:

```
$ hostname
agh
```

Run container_demo without any options. The flags variable sent to the container()
function will be zero and neither the PID namespace nor the UTS namespace are
invoked. We pass */bin/hostname* as an argument at the end of the command-line
which shows the hostname that the forked process sees:

```
$ sudo ./container_demo root/ /bin/hostname
emx
```

We can see that the hostname in the container has been duly set to "emx" but we
can see that it has also been changed on the host:

```
$ hostname
emx
```

This is because we issued the sethostbyname() system call in the root namespace and
so set the hostname for the system itself. Before we proceed, change the system's
hostname back:

```
$ sudo hostname agh
```

Run the container_demo again, but this time with the -u flag:

```
$ sudo ./container_demo root/ -u /bin/hostname
emx
```

As with the previous example, sethostbyname() has set the hostname to "emx". This
time when we check the host, we can see that the hostname has been preserved in
the root namespace:

```
$ hostname
agh
```

Now we will look at the PID namespace. Make a note of the inode of the *root*
directory:

```
$ ls -di root
10240432 root
```

Run container_demo with just the -u option so that we protect the root UTS namespace but do not invoke the PID namespace (at this stage):

```
$ ./container_demo -u root/
/ #
```

The prompt tells us we are in the / directory of the container, but we verify this by checking the contents:

```
/ # ls
bin     dev     lib       proc    sbin   usr    var.tar
boot    etc     linuxrc   root    sys    var
```

In the run_proc(), procfs is mounted just before the execl() system call. Verify this with the mount command:

```
/ # mount
proc on /proc type proc (rw,relatime)
```

If we look at the contents of the *proc* directory we see many subdirectories:

```
$ ls /proc
1       16      20520   2154    30     78      kallsyms
10      16498   20553   2157    3036   8       kcore
1026    16748   2058    2158    3096   895     keys
1078    16761   20582   2159    31     9       key-users
  :
  :
```

For brevity, we truncate the output from the command. We focus on the subdirectories that have numerical names and which correspond to running processes. The reason there are so many is because these are all the processes that are running on the system. The ps command also shows the running processes (again, for brevity we truncate the output):

```
/ # ps
PID   USER     TIME    COMMAND
   1 root       0:06   {systemd} /sbin/init splash
   2 root       0:00   [kthreadd]
   3 root       0:00   [ksoftirqd/0]
   5 root       0:00   [kworker/0:0H]
   7 root       1:11   [rcu_sched]
   8 root       0:00   [rcu_bh]
  :
  :
```

We can see that the process with PID value of 1 is the system's init process. Exit from the shell, and start up container_demo again, but this time run it with -p flag:

```
/ #
$ sudo ./container_demo -pu root/
```

We can see that there appears to far fewer processes running on the system (only two) and that our shell process has PID 1 rather than the init process:

```
/ # ps
PID    USER        TIME   COMMAND
  1 root          0:00 sh
  7 root          0:00 ps
```

We leave it up to the reader to verify the number of subdirectories under /proc with numerical names reflects the processes running in this namespace. It is important to note, that while a process running in a particular (non-root) namespace is assigned a PID from a separate (but overlapping) ID range, it is also assigned a PID from the root namespace. We demonstrate this by running a network time protocol server (ntpd) in the container:

```
/ # ntpd -l
```

Check the PID (in this case, it is 3):

```
/ # ps
PID    USER        TIME   COMMAND
  1 root          0:00 sh
  3 root          0:00 ntpd -l
  4 root          0:00 ps
```

Now on the host, check for the ntpd process:

```
$ ps -e | grep ntpd
 5836 ?           00:00:00 ntpd
```

We can see that, in the root namespace, the ntpd process has a PID of 5836. In this case, ntpd has a different PID in the root namespace than in the PID namespace of our container. It is important to understand that the PIDs could have been the same, though this would have been an unlikely coincidence. What is important to take away from this, is that the PIDs are from different ranges.

In a subsection below we cover network namespaces. While we have an NTP server running we show that there is no network isolation as we can query the server running in the container from the host:

```
$ ntpdate -q 127.0.0.1
server 127.0.0.1, stratum 1, offset 0.000024, delay
```

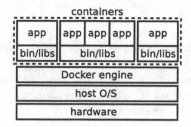

Fig. 3.1 Docker containers

```
0.02776
22 Aug 18:48:38 ntpdate[5954]: adjust time server
127.0.0.1 offset 0.000024 se
```

3.2 Docker

Docker is a *container* technology. Shipping an application to disparate systems requires that those systems support a particular set of dependencies (utilities and shared-libraries, for example). New packages have to be installed if these dependencies are absent. This could contaminate the system's existing environment and result in other applications breaking. Wrapping an application in a container along with its own environment ensures that the application is *shipped* with the correct dependencies while, at the same time, protecting the current host's environment (Fig. 3.1). In this book, we use Docker in two ways:

- Building software. Docker provides a means of automating software builds (with Dockerfiles and accompanying shell scripts). It also ensures replicable build environments.
- Testing. There are a number of steps to building an embedded systems. We use Docker as *light-weight* virtual machine for testing the system at various stages of the build.

3.2.1 Installing Docker

In this next subsection we describe how to install Docker in preparation for using it in later chapters. While there is a Docker Enterprise Edition, the Docker Community Edition (CE) for Ubuntu serves our purpose. In order to allow Apt to use repositories over HTTPS, install the following packages and configure cryptography keys:

```
$ sudo apt-get -y install apt-transport-https \
```

```
> ca-certificates curl
$ curl -fsSL \
> https://download.docker.com/linux/ubuntu/gpg | \
> sudo apt-key add -
$ sudo add-apt-repository "deb [arch=amd64] \
> https://download.docker.com/linux/ubuntu  \
> $(lsb_release -cs) stable"
```

Install Docker using the package manager:

```
$ sudo apt-get update
$ sudo apt-get -y install docker-ce
```

Add your user account (substitute "aholt" for you own username) to the docker group:

```
$ sudo usermod -a -G docker aholt
```

3.2.2   A Simple Docker Example

In this subsection, we show how to use Docker with a simple example, namely, running the date command in a Docker container. Docker containers are created from Docker images. We download a pre-built image from the Docker hub:

```
$ docker pull busybox
```

This image is based upon Busybox. View the image details with:

```
$ docker images busybox
REPOSITORY    TAG      IMAGE ID      CREATED      SIZE
busybox       latest   efe10ee6727f  2 weeks ago  1.13MB
```

We run the date command *in* the Docker container:

```
$ docker run busybox date
Thu Aug 17 14:16:44 UTC 2017
```

The docker run command created a container from the busybox image. The date command was executed and gave the expected output. It can be seen that the resultant output from the command has a timezone of UTC. If we run the date command directly on the host, we can see that (in our case) the timezone is BST:

```
$ date
```

```
Thu 17 Aug 15:16:46 BST 2017
```

This shows that the two date commands were executed in separate environments. Obviously, if your host is set for the UTC timezone, the difference will not be apparent. Check that the container is running using the docker ps command:

```
$ docker ps -a
CONTAINER ID    IMAGE          COMMAND         CREATED
STATUS                         PORTS           NAMES
e985d2e1f02c    busybox        "date"          7 minutes ago
Exited (0) 5 minutes ago                       competent_nobel
```

The docker ps command shows that the container status is "Exited". Despite this, the container still exists. If we execute the docker run command again, a second container is created:

```
$ docker run  --name="utcdate" busybox date
Thu Aug 17 14:24:01 UTC 2017
$ docker ps -a
CONTAINER ID    IMAGE          COMMAND         CREATED
STATUS          PORTS                          NAMES
43627eba3cf7    busybox        "date"          10 seconds ago
Exited (0) 9 seconds ago                       utcdate
e985d2e1f02c    busybox        "date"          7 minutes ago
Exited (0) 7 minutes ago                       competent_nobel
```

In the example above, we used the --name option to give the container an explicit name. We can start a container with the --rm option, which deletes the container when it exits:

```
$ docker run --rm busybox date
Thu Aug 17 14:30:53 UTC 2017
```

Notice, a third container has not appeared in the container list because it was removed when it exited:

```
$ docker ps -a
CONTAINER ID    IMAGE          COMMAND         CREATED
STATUS          PORTS                          NAMES
43627eba3cf7    busybox        "date"          6 minutes ago
Exited (0) 6 minutes ago                       utcdate
e985d2e1f02c    busybox        "date"          14 minutes ago
Exited (0) 14 minutes ago                      competent_nobel
```

The initial two busybox containers can be deleted with the `docker rm` command. Containers can be referenced, either by their ID or name. For illustration, we remove the containers using both methods:

```
$ docker rm e985d2e1f02c utcdate
e985d2e1f02c
utcdate
```

We leave it to the reader to verify the containers have actually been deleted. The reader should also check that, while the containers have been removed, the Busybox image still exists.

3.2.3 Building a Docker Image

In this section we show how software can be built and distributed in containers. We use a simple arcade game written in Python. The game is called Raspberry Fly (rfly) and was originally designed to run on a Raspberry Pi (although it can run on other systems) in a 80x24 console terminal window. The computer "graphics" are rendered using the Ncurses library. A Docker image for rfly already exists and is available on Docker Hub. Run the rfly game by creating a container:

```
$ docker run -it --rm agholt/rfly
```

As this is the first time the container has been run, its image is not on the local host and Docker initially reports:

```
Unable to find image 'agholt/rfly:latest' locally
```

It is not necessary to do an explicit `docker pull` of the image, Docker does this automatically. The output for the command continues, thus:

```
latest: Pulling from agholt/rfly
Digest: sha256:a3973a87e6d4eae7bb7d12f25a87ede7023f...
Status: Downloaded newer image for agholt/rfly:latest
```

Figure 3.2 shows the banner screen for the game. After a few seconds a menu screen appears inviting you to play the game (or quit). Verify (in a separate terminal window) that the image has downloaded:

```
$ docker images emx/rfly
REPOSITORY   TAG      IMAGE ID      CREATED         SIZE
agholt/rfly  latest   853dbc2df4aa  9 minutes ago   158MB
```

Here, we describe the steps required to create this Docker image. Make a subdirectory to work in:

```
$ mkdir ~/emxbook/rfly && cd ~/emxbook/rfly
```

The Python source code for the game is in the git repository we cloned earlier. Untar *Rfly.tar.gz* in the current directory:

```
$ tar zxf ../emx/chapter3/Rfly.tar.gz .
```

This creates the directory, *Rfly*, which contains the files for the source code of rfly:

```
$ cd Rfly/
```

Create a source distribution with sdist:

```
$ python setup.py sdist
```

This results in a compressed tarball in the *dist* directory:

```
$ ls dist
fly-0.2.tar.gz
```

We need to build an initial image for Python and for that we need a Dockerfile. A Dockerfile is a configuration file with the instructions on how to build an image. The Dockerfile Listing 3.5 describes how we build our initial image.

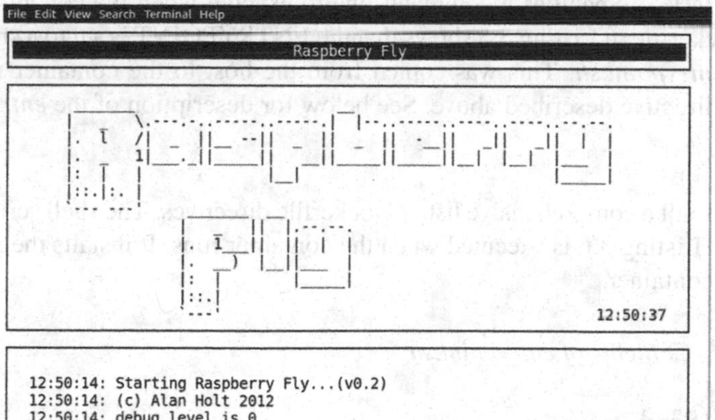

Fig. 3.2 Raspberry fly banner screenshot

Listing 3.5 *Contents of Dockerfile*

```
FROM jgoerzen/debian-base-minimal

ENV PATH /usr/local/bin:$PATH
ENV HOME /opt

RUN apt-get update && apt-get upgrade -y && \
    apt-get -y install python

WORKDIR /opt
COPY Rfly/dist/fly-0.2.tar.gz /opt/fly-0.2.tar.gz
COPY entrypoint.sh /opt/entrypoint.sh

ENTRYPOINT ["./entrypoint.sh"]
```

The Dockerfile uses a number of directives which are described below:

FROM: Docker images can be built from scratch but it is typical to base them on an existing image. The FROM directive specifies that the image we are creating is based upon a minimal Debian image. If the image is not cached on the host, then Docker downloads the image from the Docker Hub repository at build time.

ENV: Sets environment variables within the container.

RUN: Instructs Docker to execute a command in a new layer over the current layer. The result of the command is committed to a new image which is used for the next step of the Dockerfile.

WORKDIR: The WORKDIR directive sets the current working directory for the other directives in the Dockerfile.

COPY: Copy files from the system host to the container.

ENTRYPOINT: Specifies a command-line to execute when the container is run. The Dockerfile in Listing 3.5 shows that the ENTRYPOINT is set to a shell script called *entrypoint.sh*. This was copied from the host to the container using the COPY directive described above. See below for description of the *entrypoint.sh* script.

Note, this is not a comprehensive list of Dockerfile directives. The shell script, *entrypoint.sh*, in Listing 3.6 is executed when the container runs. It installs the rfly game within the container.

Listing 3.6 *Contents of entrypoint.sh*

```
#!/bin/bash

set -e

cd /opt
```

```
tar zxf fly-0.2.tar.gz
cd fly-0.2/

python setup.py install
```

Build the image rfly-bld:v0:

```
docker build -t rfly-bld:v0 .
```

Verify the image exists:

```
$ docker images rfly-bld
REPOSITORY   TAG      IMAGE ID       CREATED         SIZE
rfly-bld     v0       b459bda0fc36   5 seconds ago   157MB
```

Create a container, rfly-bld by running the image python-bld:

```
$ docker run --name="rfly-bld" rfly-bld:v0
```

When the container runs, it executes the *entrypoint.sh* shell script which installs the rfly game within the container. Once *entrypoint.sh* has completed, the container exits. We can see that a container exists with the docker ps command:

```
$ docker ps -a
CONTAINER ID     IMAGE          COMMAND                  
CREATED          STATUS                         PORTS
NAMES
86822af4cb6f     rfly-bld:v0    "/bin/sh -c ./entr..."
12 seconds ago   Exited (0) 14 seconds ago
rfly-bld
```

The rfly-bld container was created purely for the purpose of installing the rfly game. The installed game exists within the rfly-bld container but not in the rfly-bld:v0 image upon which rfly-bld is based. We need to build a new image from the rfly-bld container. We do this with the docker commit command:

```
$ docker commit rfly-bld rfly-bld:v1
sha256:6b0f916e56ac64ef4e4c2904504e5f175e1266c116bcf...
```

An image called rfly-bld:v1 is created from the container, rfly-bld:

```
$ docker images rfly-bld:v1
```

```
REPOSITORY    TAG      IMAGE ID       CREATED         SIZE
rfly-bld      v1       6b0f916e56ac   10 seconds ago  158MB
```

The container, rfly-bld, has now served its purpose, we can delete it:

```
$ docker rm rfly-bld
```

Using the rfly-bld image as a base, we build an image, rfly. For this we use a Dockerfile called *Dockerfile.rfly*, the contents of which are shown in Listing 3.7. The purpose of *Dockerfile.rfly* is simple, it just sets the ENTRYPOINT for the container to the pathname of the rfly game.

Listing 3.7 *Contents of Dockerfile*

```
FROM rfly-bld

ENTRYPOINT ["/usr/local/bin/rfly"]
```

Build the rfly image and verify it has been created:

```
$ docker build -t rfly -f Dockerfile.rfly .
$ docker images rfly
REPOSITORY    TAG      IMAGE ID       CREATED         SIZE
rfly          latest   e44af7e4bd2c   10 minutes ago  158MB
```

This rfly image is essentially the agholt/rfly image from Docker Hub. The game is ready to play using:

```
$ docker run -it --rm rfly
```

Finally, we can tidy up by removing the rfly-bld images:

```
$ docker rmi rfly-bld:v0 rfly-bld:1
```

3.2.4 DHCP Server Example

Here, we present another Docker example but we also take the opportunity to cover some other topics, namely, *network namespaces*. We covered namespaces in Sect. 3.1 but restricted our discussion to PID namespaces and UTS namespaces. We return to the "container" example from Sect. 3.1 and run it in a network namespace. We set up a DHCP server running in a Docker container. We will use the DHCP server to set the IP details of the namespace. To do this, we need to connect the Docker

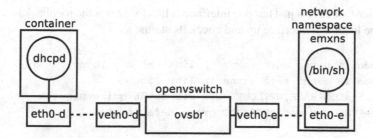

Fig. 3.3 A DHCP server in a Docker container

container (running the DHCP server) and the network namespace to some network switch. Rather than a physical switch, we use an Open vSwitch which is a software switch abstraction commonly used in SDN (software defined networks) [4].

Return to the ~/*emxbook/* directory:

```
$ cd ~/emxbook/
```

Figure 3.3 shows how our virtual network is set up. At the centre is an Open vSwitch bridge (ovsbr). Install Open vSwitch:

```
$ sudo apt-get install openvswitch-switch
```

Create the ovsbr Open vSwitch bridge:

```
$ sudo ovs-vsctl add-br ovsbr
```

The ovsbr bridge is connected to the network namespace and the Docker container by a couple of virtual Ethernet (veth) pairs (veth0-e/eth0-e and veth0-d/eth0-d). Veth pairs can be viewed as two (virtual) Ethernet interfaces connected by a virtual patch cable.

Create a network namespace, emxns:

```
$ sudo ip netns add emxns
```

Check the state interface within emxns by running a command within the namespace:

```
$ sudo ip netns exec emxns ip link list
1: lo: <LOOPBACK> mtu 65536 qdisc noop state DOWN mode
DEFAULT group default qlen 1
    link/loopback 00:00:00:00:00:00 brd 00:00:00:00:00:00
```

We can see that emxns just has one interface called lo. This is the loopback interface.
Bring the loopback interface up and check its status:

```
$ sudo ip netns exec emxns ip link set dev lo up
$ sudo ip netns exec emxns ip link list
1: lo: <LOOPBACK,UP,LOWER_UP> mtu 65536 qdisc noqueue
state UNKNOWN mode DEFAULT group default qlen 1
```

Create a pair of virtual Ethernet (type veth) interfaces:

```
$ sudo ip link add veth0-e type veth peer name eth0-e
```

Both interfaces are (initially) created in the root namespace. We attach eth0-e (and,
thus, removing it from the root namespace) to emxns:

```
$ sudo ip link set eth0-e netns emxns
```

Bring up the eth0-e interface and verify its status:

```
$ sudo ip netns exec emxns ip link set dev eth0-e up
$ sudo ip netns exec emxns ip link list eth0-e
7: eth0-e@if8: <BROADCAST,MULTICAST,UP,LOWER_UP> mtu
1500 qdisc noqueue state UP mode DEFAULT group default
qlen 1000
    link/ether 66:74:a8:8d:21:ee brd ff:ff:ff:ff:ff:ff
link-netnsid 0
```

The interface veth0-e, will remain in the root namespace (and will connect to the
ovsbr bridge). Bring it up with the command-line:

```
$ sudo ip link set dev veth0-e up
```

Create a veth pair for the Docker container that will run dhcpd:

```
$ sudo ip link add veth0-d type veth peer name eth0-d
```

Bring up the two interfaces:

```
$ sudo ip link set dev veth0-d up
$ sudo ip link set dev eth0-d up
```

Assign an IP address (and subnet mask) to eth0-d:

```
$ sudo ifconfig eth0-d 192.168.1.6 netmask 255.255.255.0
```

Add the interfaces veth0-e and veth0-d to the ovsbr:

```
$ sudo ovs-vsctl add-port ovsbr veth0-e
$ sudo ovs-vsctl add-port ovsbr veth0-d
```

Verify the switch and its interfaces:

```
$ sudo ovs-vsctl show
3952e2d4-c16a-42d1-921a-54ed59dfa386
    Bridge ovsbr
        Port ovsbr
            Interface ovsbr
                type: internal
        Port "veth0-d"
            Interface "veth0-d"
        Port "veth0-e"
            Interface "veth0-e"
    ovs_version: "2.5.2"
```

Download the repository for the DHCP server Docker container:

```
$ git clone \
> https://github.com/networkboot/docker-dhcpd.git
$ cd docker-dhcpd
```

Build the image (and verify):

```
$ docker build -t emx/dhcpd .
$ docker images emx/dhcpd
REPOSITORY   TAG      IMAGE ID       CREATED       SIZE
emx/dhcpd    latest   2cb162b4f386   4 hours ago   132MB
```

Create the directory, *data*:

```
$ mkdir data
```

In the *data* directory, create the file *dhcpd.conf* with contents shown in Listing 3.8.

Listing 3.8 *Contents of* dhcpd.conf

```
subnet 192.168.1.0 netmask 255.255.255.0 {
        option routers                   192.168.1.1;
```

```
            option subnet-mask                  255.255.255.0;

            option domain-name                  "emx.local";
            option domain-name-servers          8.8.8.8;

        range 192.168.1.20 192.168.1.100;
    }
```

Set the following options:

```
$ unset OPTS
$ OPTS[0]="-it"
$ OPTS[1]="--rm"
$ OPTS[2]="--net host"
$ OPTS[3]="-v `pwd`/data:/data"
$ OPTS[4]="emx/dhcpd"
```

Start the DHCP server by running the container:

```
$ docker run ${OPTS[*]} eth0-d
Internet Systems Consortium DHCP Server 4.3.3
Copyright 2004-2015 Internet Systems Consortium.
All rights reserved.
For info, please visit https://www.isc.org/software/dhcp/
Config file: /data/dhcpd.conf
Database file: /data/dhcpd.leases
PID file: /var/run/dhcpd.pid
Wrote 2 leases to leases file.
Listening on LPF/eth0-d/e2:0e:0b:86:64:1d/192.168.1.0/24
Sending on   LPF/eth0-d/e2:0e:0b:86:64:1d/192.168.1.0/24
Sending on   Socket/fallback/fallback-net
Server starting service.
```

The DHCP server is now running in the foreground, so from a different terminal window, request IP details from the DHCP server:

```
$ sudo ip netns exec emxns dhclient eth0-e
```

When we issue the dhclient command above, we see the DHCP DORA exchange from dhcpd server:

```
DHCPDISCOVER from aa:d3:00:d2:61:d0 via eth0-d
DHCPOFFER on 192.168.1.24 to aa:d3:00:d2:61:d0 (agh)
via eth0-d
```

```
DHCPREQUEST for 192.168.1.24 (192.168.1.6) from
aa:d3:00:d2:61:d0 (agh) via eth0-d
DHCPACK on 192.168.1.24 to aa:d3:00:d2:61:d0 (agh) via
eth0-d
```

Now run container_demo within a PID, UTS *and* network namespace:

```
$ sudo ip netns exec emxns ./container_demo -pu root/
/ # hostname        # check the hostname
emx
```

Check that the container has an IP address:

```
/ # ifconfig eth0-e
eth0-e Link encap:Ethernet  HWaddr 66:74:A8:8D:21:EE
        inet addr:192.168.1.24  Bcast:192.168.1.255
Mask:255.255.255.0
        inet6 addr: fe80::6474:a8ff:fe8d:21ee/64
Scope:Link
        UP BROADCAST RUNNING MULTICAST  MTU:1500
Metric:1
        RX packets:94 errors:0 dropped:0 overruns:0
frame:0
        TX packets:41 errors:0 dropped:0 overruns:0
carrier:0
        collisions:0 txqueuelen:1000
        RX bytes:11320 (11.0 KiB)  TX bytes:3514
(3.4 KiB)
```

We can see that the DHCP server did indeed serve the IP address details for eth0-e in the emxns namespace. Verify the container can communicate by pinging the DHCP server:

```
/ # ping -c 4 192.168.1.6
PING 192.168.1.6 (192.168.1.6): 56 data bytes
64 bytes from 192.168.1.6: seq=0 ttl=64 time=0.875 ms
64 bytes from 192.168.1.6: seq=1 ttl=64 time=0.248 ms
64 bytes from 192.168.1.6: seq=2 ttl=64 time=0.272 ms
64 bytes from 192.168.1.6: seq=3 ttl=64 time=0.308 ms

--- 192.168.1.6 ping statistics ---
4 packets transmitted, 4 packets received, 0% packet
loss
round-trip min/avg/max = 0.248/0.425/0.875 ms
```

As one last test, we repeat the NTP example given in Sect. 3.1.2. Start the NTP
daemon in emxns:

```
/ # ntpd -1
```

If we try to access ntpd using the localhost address (127.0.0.1) from the root namespace, we get the error message below:

```
$ ntpdate -q 127.0.0.1
server 127.0.0.1, stratum 0, offset 0.000000, delay
0.00000
22 Aug 19:37:23 ntpdate[6796]: no server suitable for
synchronization found
```

The ntpd server is isolated in the emxns network namespace. To access it, we need
to reference it by the IP address on eth0-e:

```
$ ntpdate -q 192.168.1.24
server 192.168.1.24, stratum 1, offset 0.000020, delay
0.02785
22 Aug 19:50:30 ntpdate[6909]: adjust time server
192.168.1.24 offset 0.000020 sec
```

3.3 Summary

In this chapter we have looked at the underlying kernel technology behind containers. Namespace are abstract system resources so that processes running within them
are isolated from each other. Docker is a popular open-source container technology which we use in later chapters to build embedded operating system software.
Building large software systems is problematic due to the number of dependencies.
When development teams are distributed, replicating their environments so that they
have the correct dependencies is difficult. Docker containers ensure environments
are reproducible across systems. Docker images can be shared using the Docker
Hub registry. Container builds can be automated with Dockerfiles. Although we
have not covered them in this book, whole container ecosystems can be managed
using sophisticated orchestration applications. For our purposes, the simple Docker
command-line utilities are sufficient for the examples in this book.

References

1. Miell I, Sayers AH (2016) Docker in practice. Manning Publications Company
2. Goasguen S (2015) Docker cookbook. O'Reilly Media Incorporated
3. Nickoloff J (2016) Docker in action, 1st edn. Manning Publications Co., Greenwich, CT, USA
4. Channegowda M, Nejabati R, Simeonidou D (2013) Software-defined optical networks technology and infrastructure: enabling software-defined optical network operations. J Opt Commun Netw 5(10):A274–A282

The Filesystem in Detail   4

Persistent data is stored in files. Files may contain text, database records, source code or executable instructions, but as far as the kernel is concerned, the content of a file is merely an unstructured byte stream. Files are organised in *directories*. Directories themselves are files but, unlike "regular" files, the kernel imposes a structure on their content. Directories contain a list of *links* to files (and other directories) in the filesystem. A collection of files and directories, along with associated *meta data* form a *filesystem*.

Files that store user data are sometimes called *regular files* in order to distinguish them from other file objects in the filesystem. In addition to regular files and directories, other file objects can be accessed through the filesystem:

Device files: A device file or *special* file is a device driver interface. Device files can be accessed through standard I/O calls in the same way as a regular file even though the hardware the driver controls may not be a storage device.

FIFO: FIFOs (first in first out) or named pipes are file objects used for interprocess communication (IPC).

Unix domain sockets: A Unix domain socket is an IPC mechanism similar to a FIFO. Sockets are created and managed with the same systems calls used for network sockets.

Symbolic links: Symbolic links (also called soft links) overcome the limitation of hard links which cannot link to files across filesystem boundaries.

A filesystem is divided into blocks (typically between 512 and 4096 bytes in size). Blocks are allocated for storing the content of files and directories. Some blocks are reserved for meta data and information about the filesystem itself. Physical disk drives can be divided into (one or more) *partitions* and filesystems are allocated to partitions. In this chapter we will examine the filesystems in detail. We discuss the organisation of physical disks and how filesystems are mapped to disk partitions.

© Springer International Publishing AG, part of Springer Nature 2018
A. Holt and C.-Y. Huang, *Embedded Operating Systems*, Undergraduate
Topics in Computer Science, https://doi.org/10.1007/978-3-319-72977-0_4

4.1 GNU/Linux File Space

While primary storage (main memory) is accessible directly from a running program, secondary storage is only accessible through kernel services. The part of the kernel that provides these services is called the filesystem. The purpose of the kernel filesystem services is to present a common interface to the file space such that the complexities of the hardware are hidden from the programmer/user:

- Unix operating systems can implement the file space over a number of separate filesystems.
- Unix filesystems are sometimes referred to as *demountable volumes* [1] as they can be dynamically added and removed from the file space.
- GNU/Linux supports many different filesystem types using a virtual filesystem (VFS).
- GNU/Linux supports a variety of physical storage devices such as hard disks and solid state devices.
- Physical storage devices can be partitioned to support multiple filesystems.

We will discuss filesystems, VFS and partitions in more detail later in the chapter. In this section we will focus on the file space as viewed by the user. From the users' perspective, the structure of the filesystem and organisation of disk partitions is transparent.

Even a small embedded GNU/Linux system will have a large number of files. It is important then, that the filesystem provides some method of organising files. Unix uses the concept of a *directory* to group files. Not only can regular files be grouped into directories but also other directories (subdirectories). The Unix file space resembles an inverted hierarchical tree. Below, we introduce some Unix terms regarding directories:

Root directory: The directory at the top of the file space hierarchy is called the root directory which is referenced by a forward slash "/".

Current/working directory: User's work within a directory. This is called the *current* or *working* directory. The current directory can be changed at any time during the user's session (typically with the cd command). Every directory has a directory entry which is a link to itself called "." which is a way of referring to the current directory. It is useful when using commands like cp (copy) which requires both a source file and a destination file/directory as parameters. For example, if we need to copy a file into the current directory, we use the command-line:

```
$ cp /tmp/tmpfile.txt .
```

Parent directory: Every directory has a directory entry called ".." which is (with the exception of root) a link to the directory above. Root does have ".." directory entry but it is merely a link to itself (just like ".").

Home directory: Each user is assigned a home directory. When a user first logs in the current directory is set to the home directory.

As we have seen, file objects are given names. A file object name must be unique within its own directory, but need not be unique throughout the entire file space. A file is referenced by both its name and its location within the file space. Files are located using a list of directory names which describes a "path" through the directory hierarchy to the file. This list of directories followed by the file name itself is called the *pathname* of the file. Pathnames can either be absolute or relative. Absolute pathnames begin with a "/" and describe the path to the file from the root directory. Relative pathnames, on the other hand, do not start with a "/" and describe a path to a file from the user's current directory. For example, the kernel header file *ipv6.h* is located in the directory */usr/include/linux*. Note that the "/" is also used as a delimiter between directories. For example, we can reference the file *ipv6.h* by its absolute pathname:

```
$ ls /usr/include/linux/ipv6.h
/usr/include/linux/ipv6.h
```

The absolute pathname is the same regardless of the user's current directory. Relative pathname references begin at the the user's current directory. For example, make */usr* the current directory:

```
$ cd /usr
```

Reference *ipv6.h* using a relative pathname:

```
$ ls include/linux/ipv6.h
include/linux/ipv6.h
```

If we were in our home directory (which is, say */home/aholt*), the relative pathname to the *ipv6.h* is different:

```
$ cd      # change to home directory
$ ls ../../usr/include/linux//ipv6.h
../../usr/include/linux//ipv6.h
```

Notice how we use the ".." notation to reference the parent directory. The choice of absolute or relative pathnames depends which is most convenient to use.

4.2   Permissions

Permissions determine how users can access files. A user may be entitled to read, write or execute a file, depending upon the type of user they are and the permissions that apply to them. Unix defines three types of user with respect to file access:

Owner: Each file has one and only one owner. Typically, this is the user that created the file but it is possible to change the file's ownership.
Group: User can belong to various groups which are defined in the file */etc/group*.
Other: Users that are neither the owner of the file nor a member of its group can access the file according to the "other" permissions.

Permissions set for the owner override those for the group and group permission override those for other. Owners and groups have a designated user (owner) and group ID which are called the uid and gid respectively. The command-line below shows the user name and uid along with the group name and gid:

```
$ stat -c '%N user: %U/%u group: %G/%g' ~/.profile
'/home/aholt/.profile' user aholt/1000 group aholt/1000
```

Each user type (owner, group or other) are assigned permissions, namely, read, write and execute. A permission is enabled if the corresponding permission bit it set to 1. Similarly it is disabled if the permission bit is set to 0. File permissions are represented as a 9-bit pattern of an integer field (in the file's inode). The least significant three bits are the user permissions for other (read, write and execute). The three most significant bits are the owners permissions and the middle three bits are for the group. Each three bit grouping yields an octal value which describes the files permissions for the respective user type. Table 4.1 shows the octal values of each permission.

Table 4.1 File permissions

Octal value	Comment
0001	Other can execute
0002	Other can write
0004	Other can read
0010	Group can execute
0020	Group can write
0040	Group can read
0100	Owner can execute
0200	Owner can write
0400	Owner can read

We demonstrate file permissions with an example. Create a temporary file:

```
$ touch /tmp/tmpfile
```

Examine the permissions of the file:

```
$ stat -c'%a %A' /tmp/tmpfile
644 -rw-r--r--
```

We can see that read and write permissions are set for the owner (0400 + 0200 = 0600) and only read permissions are granted for the group and other (0400).

In this example we add execute permission to the owner (even though it contains no executable content), write permission for the group and remove all permissions for other. Setting all the permission bits on for the owner we calculate the octal value: 0400 + 0200 + 0100 = 0700. Setting read and execute permission bits on for the group octal value is: 0400 + 0100 = 0500. For other, all the permission bits are cleared, hence, the value is 0. Change the permissions:

```
$ chmod 750 /tmp/tmpfile
```

We verify the permissions with the stat command:

```
$ stat -c'%a %A' /tmp/tmpfile
750 -rwxr-x---
```

4.3 Other File Objects

Unix operating systems adopt a philosophy "everything is a file". As mentioned earlier, file objects are not just confined to regular files and directories. In this subsection we will discuss, with examples, the other file objects found within the filesystem. The list below serves as a reminder of these file objects:

- Device files (special files)
- FIFOs (named pipes)
- Unix domain sockets
- Symbolic links

4.3.1   Device Files

Device files are input/output interfaces to device drivers. Just like regular files, device files have directory entries and inodes but unlike regular files, devices are not allocated blocks on any disk (other than for their inode).

There are two type of device files, namely, character and block. Character devices are devices which send and receive raw streams of data. Serial lines and printers are examples of character devices. Whereas character devices can transfer data one character at time, block devices transfer data in blocks. Block devices are typically file storage devices, for example hard disks or solid state devices. The command-line below shows examples of both types:

```
$ stat -c '%N %F' /dev/ttyS0 /dev/sda1
'/dev/ttyS0' character special file
'/dev/sda1' block special file
```

The */dev/ttyS0* device is the host serial port and is, therefore, a character device. The */dev/sda1* is a block device because it is a filesystem partition. Devices files also have *major* and *minor* numbers. The major number identifies the device driver type and the minor number specifies the instance of the device. For example, */dev/ttyS0* and */dev/ttyS1* are both serial devices and have the same major number, which is 4 (because the same driver code is used to control both devices). They have minor number of 40 and 41 respectively in order to distinguish between the two interfaces:

```
$ stat -c'%N major: %t, minor: %T' /dev/ttyS[01]
'/dev/ttyS0' major: 4, minor: 40
'/dev/ttyS1' major: 4, minor: 41
```

In this subsection we will demonstrate the concept of a device file by writing a rudimentary device driver. We will write the driver as a loadable module. Listing 4.1 shows the source code for the dummy device driver *ddev.c*. It comprises two functions: dd_init() and dd_cleanup() which are run when we load the module and unload the module respectively.

Listing 4.2 shows the source code for the include file *dd_fops.h*. This defines the functions that enable the programmer to interact with the driver, albeit that interaction is limited as only open and close operations are defined. Nevertheless, this is sufficient to demonstrate how we can access a device file just as we would with any regular file.

Listing 4.1 *ddev.c*

```
/* ddev.c */

#include <linux/module.h>
#include <linux/kernel.h>
```

```
#include <linux/init.h>
#include <linux/fs.h>

#include "dd_fops.h"

/* dummy device initialisation function */
int dd_init(void)
{
    int ret;


    ret = register_chrdev(dd_major, DEV, &dd_fops);
    if (ret < 0) {
        printk(KERN_WARNING \
                    "ddev: unable to assign major\n");
        return dd_major;
    }

    if (dd_major==0) dd_major = ret;

    printk(KERN_DEBUG \
                "assigned major number %d\n", dd_major);
    printk(KERN_DEBUG \
                    "initialised dummy device driver\n");

    return 0;
}

/* dummy device cleanup function */
void dd_cleanup(void)
{
    unregister_chrdev(dd_major, DEV);
    printk(KERN_DEBUG \
                    "removing dummy device driver\n");
}


module_init(dd_init);
module_exit(dd_cleanup);

MODULE_LICENSE("GPL");
```

Listing 4.2 *dd_fops.h*

```c
/* dd_fops.h */

#define DEV "ddev"

static int dd_major = 256;
static int dd_minor;

/* dummy device open function */
static int dd_open(struct inode *in, struct file *fp)
{
    dd_minor = (MINOR(in->i_rdev)&0x0f);
    printk(KERN_INFO "ddev: open %d\n", dd_minor);
    try_module_get(THIS_MODULE);
    return 0;
}

/* dummy device close function */
static int dd_close(struct inode *in, struct file *fp)
{
    module_put(THIS_MODULE);
    dd_minor = (MINOR(in->i_rdev)&0x0f);
    printk(KERN_INFO "ddev: closed %d\n", dd_minor);
    return 0;
}

struct file_operations dd_fops = {
    .open =  dd_open,
    .release = dd_close
};
```

We compile the ddev module using the make utility. Listing 4.3 shows the content of *Makefile*.

Listing 4.3 *Makefile*

```
obj-m   := ddev.o
KDIR    := /lib/modules/$(shell uname -r)/build
PWD := $(shell pwd)

all:
    $(MAKE) -C $(KDIR) M=$(PWD) modules
```

```
clean:
    $(MAKE) -C $(KDIR) M=$(PWD) clean
```

Compile the module by running make:

```
$ make
make -C /lib/modules/2.6.32-26-generic-pae/build
M=/home/aholt/development/lbook/fs modules
make[1]: Entering directory
'/usr/src/linux-headers-2.6.32-26-generic-pae'
  CC [M]  /home/aholt/development/lbook/fs/ddev.o
  Building modules, stage 2.
  MODPOST 1 modules
  CC       /home/aholt/development/lbook/fs/ddev.mod.o
  LD [M]   /home/aholt/development/lbook/fs/ddev.ko
make[1]: Leaving directory
'/usr/src/linux-headers-2.6.32-26-generic-pae'
```

A successful compilation produces the module file *ddev.ko* which can be loaded into
the kernel:

```
$ sudo insmod ddev.ko
```

Confirm the module has been loaded:

```
$ lsmod | grep ddev
ddev                    1412  0
```

Check the end of the kernel buffering to see the messages output by the ddev module:

```
$ dmesg | tail -n2
[20268.989854] assigned major number 256
[20268.989856] initialised dummy device driver
```

Find the assigned major number:

```
$ grep ddev /proc/devices
256 ddev
```

We create two instances of ddev in the */dev* directory. While they have the same
major number (same driver code) they have different minor numbers:

```
$ sudo mknod /dev/ddev0 c 256 0
$ sudo mknod /dev/ddev1 c 256 1
```

Next we write a utility, ddio, to run in user space to access the driver. The only system calls that the ddio command makes are to open() and close() because these are the only operations ddev supports. The source code for *ddio.c* shown in Listing 4.4.

Listing 4.4 *Source code for ddio.c*

```
#include <fcntl.h>
#include <stdio.h>

main(int argc, char *argv[])
{

    int fd;

    if((fd = open(argv[1], O_RDONLY)) < 0) {
        perror("error opening file");
        return -1;
    }

    printf("hit any key to close %s\n", argv[1]);
    getchar();

    close(fd);
}
```

Compile *ddio.c*:

```
$ gcc -o ddio ddio.c
```

Use ddio to open the device driver

```
$ ./ddio /dev/ddev0
hit any key to close /dev/ddev0
```

The ddio command opens */dev/ddev0* and then waits for a response from the user. Meanwhile the *dev/ddev0* remains open. Check dmesg (in another terminal window) to see the kernel output:

```
$ dmesg | tail -n1
[20333.467439] ddev: open 0
```

In the window running ddio, hit any key to close */dev/ddev0*, then check dmesg:

```
$ dmesg | tail -n1
[20374.512204] ddev: closed 0
```

Finally unload the module:

```
$ sudo rmmod pport
```

The rmmod command will cause the cleanup function to run. We will leave it to the reader to check dmesg to verify that the appropriate messages have been written to the kernel console.

This exercise demonstrates that, even though device files are different to regular files, they can still be accessed using common system calls. The open() and close() systems call in *ddio.h* are called in the same way irrespective of whether the file object is a device or regular file. While ddev only supports open and close operations it could be expanded to support the other filesystem calls.

4.3.2 FIFOs and Unix Domain Sockets

FIFOs and Unix domain sockets are similar concepts so we will describe them together in this subsection. FIFOs are sometimes called named pipes because they appear as a file object within the filesystem, and so, must have a name. Unlike "unnamed" pipes, FIFOs exist after the process that created them has terminated. For example, create a FIFO *mypipe* with the command-line below:

```
$ mkfifo mypipe
```

Confirm the file type with the stat command:

```
$ stat -c'%F' mypipe
fifo
```

Write some data to the pipe with:

```
$ echo "hello" > mypipe &
[1] 3835
```

The write process above is run in background and blocks because there is no read process (yet). In order to demonstrate the first-in-first-out nature of the FIFO we execute another process (in background) to write to the pipe:

```
$ echo "world" > mypipe &
[2] 3837
```

Now we have two processes blocked in I/O. We execute a process to read from the FIFO:

```
$ cat < mypipe
hello
world
[1]-  Done                        echo "hello" > mypipe
[2]+  Done                        echo "world" > mypipe
```

Note that the data is read in the order it was written and that the write processes, that were previously blocked, complete their I/O calls (and eventually terminate).

Sockets are an API primarily designed for network applications where a client on one machine can communicate with a server on another. The sockets API also supports "local" sockets which are known as Unix domain sockets. We will demonstrate Unix domain sockets by writing a simple echo server (and client) in Python. The server program is shown in Listing 4.5. It waits for a client to initiate a connection over a Unix domain socket, which in this case, has the pathname */tmp/usocket*. Once a session has been established the server listens for any data on the socket. Any data it receives it "echoes" back to the client.

Listing 4.6 shows the Python client script. The client initiates a session to the server over (*/tmp/usocket*) and sends some data. It then waits for it to be sent back by the server.

Listing 4.5 *Echo server: Source code for echod.py*

```python
#!/usr/bin/env python

import sys,os
from socket import *

usage = "usage: %s <socketename>" % (sys.argv[0])

s = "/tmp/usocket"

if __name__=='__main__':

    u = socket(AF_UNIX, SOCK_STREAM)
```

```
    try:
        os.unlink(s)
    except OSError:
        pass

    u.bind(s)
    u.listen(1)

    c,a = u.accept()

    while 1:
        m = c.recv(1024)
        if not m: break
        c.send(m)

    c.close()
```

Listing 4.6 *Echo client: source code for echo.py*

```
#!/usr/bin/env python

import sys
from socket import *

usage = "usage: %s <string>" % (sys.argv[0])

s = "/tmp/usocket"

if __name__=='__main__':

    if sys.argv[1:] == []:
        print usage
        exit(-1)

    u = socket(AF_UNIX, SOCK_STREAM)
    u.connect(s)
    u.send(" ".join(sys.argv[1:]))
    r = u.recv(1024)
    u.close()
    print "Received: %s" % (repr(r))
```

Run the echo server as a background process:

```
$ ./echod.py &
[1] 4348
```

This will create a socket file object, which we can see with the stat command:

```
$ stat -c'%F' /tmp/usocket
socket
```

Run the echo client supplying a message we wish to send (and receive back) from the server:

```
$ ./echo.py hello world
Received: 'hello world'
[1]+  Done                        ./echod.py /tmp/usocket
```

4.3.3   Symbolic Links

A directory entry constitutes a link to a file and it is perfectly valid for a file to have multiple links. While links pointing to the same file can be in different directories, they must be on the same filesystem. It is not possible to create a *hard* link on one filesystem to a file that resides on some other filesystem. Using the */proc/uptime* file as an example, try to create a link to it in the current directory:

```
$ ln /proc/uptime uptime
ln: creating hard link 'uptime' => '/proc/uptime':
Invalid cross-device link
```

This generates an error message indicating the command failed. This is because the current directory and */proc/uptime* exist on different filesystems. A symbolic link, on the other hand, *can* be created across filesystems:

```
$ ln -s /proc/uptime uptime
```

If we compare the inode numbers of the symbolic link *./uptime* and the file */proc/uptime* we see the values are different:

```
$ ls -li uptime /proc/uptime
4026531982 -r--r--r-- 1 root  root   0 2013-05-01 14:10
/proc/uptime
   3944833 lrwxrwxrwx 1 aholt aholt 12 2013-05-01 14:09
uptime -> /proc/uptime
```

This is because *./uptime* is a separate file object to /emph/proc/uptime. If *./uptime* was a hard link (assuming it could be created) then it would have the same inode number as /emph/proc/uptime. The file types reported by the stat command, are:

```
$ stat -c'%F' uptime /proc/uptime
symbolic link
regular empty file
```

We can now access *proc/uptime* using the link *.uptime* in our current directory:

```
$ cat uptime
9928.96 17606.88
```

4.4 The Filesystem

The GNU/Linux file space comprises one or more filesystems. Unlike some operating systems, where separate filesystems are accessed by unique device identifiers, GNU/Linux filesystems are combined into a single hierarchy. GNU/Linux needs at least one filesystem which is mounted on the root directory and is referred to as the root filesystem. Subsequent filesystems can be mounted on a subdirectory. The contents of any subdirectory that is used as a filesystem *mount point* is overlayed with the contents of the mounted filesystem. The diagram in Fig. 4.1 shows partition */dev/hda1* mounted on /. The mount operation makes the root directory of */dev/hda1*, the root directory of the file hierarchy. Figure 4.1 also shows a second partition, */dev/hda2*, mounted on */home*. The root directory of the filesystem on the */dev/hda2* device becomes the */home* directory in the file hierarchy.

GNU/Linux supports over 50 types of filesystem. In order to support multiple filesystem, Linux implements a virtual filesystem (VFS). The VFS is an abstraction layer above the actual filesystem (see Fig. 4.2). Users can then access files using a common interface regardless of structure of the underlying filesystem.

The default filesystem for GNU/Linux is the Extended filesystem. The original extended filesystem (ext) has been deprecated and ext2, ext3 and ext4 are used instead. From now on, we use the generic term "ext" to mean either ext2, ext3 or ext4. The original Unix filesystem suffered scalability issues as the size of hard disks increased. High latencies resulted from disk heads moving between inodes at the start of filesystem and data blocks located at the end. The Berkeley fast filesystem (FFS) divides the filesystem into chunks, so that inodes and associated data blocks are located in the same general proximity on the disk. This helps to minimise head movement and access latency. In fact the Berkeley FFS is now considered to be the Unix filesystem (UFS) rather than the original Unix filesystem. While the original Unix filesystem has been deprecated, it is worth a short review as a number of the concepts are still applicable to many of the GNU/Linux filesystem.

The Unix filesystem is divided into equal size blocks (between 512 K and 4 M). These blocks are used to store information about the filesystems itself as well as user data. The diagram in Fig. 4.3 shows the blocks of the filesystem grouped into four areas. These areas are described below:

Bootblock: The bootblock stores a small program called a *bootloader*. This program is used to load the kernel. It is loaded into memory and execution is passed to it when the system is booted.

Superblock: Three types of information are stored in the superblock:

- Parameters which are fixed at the time of the filesystem's creation.
- Tunable parameters.
- Current state information.

Inodes: Index nodes (inodes) are data structures that contain meta data about file objects including pointers to the data blocks allocated to it.

Data blocks: The remaining blocks are allocated to file content (directories as well as regular files).

The inode is the link between a file's name and the blocks on the disk allocated to it. The inode contains the file object's meta data and pointers to the data blocks on the disk where the content is stored. In order to reference a file object, its directory entry must be fetched from the directory in which it resides. The diagram in Fig. 4.4 shows a directory entry for the file, *largefile.dat*. The inode number identifies the relevant inode on the disk. When the file is opened the inode data structure in the disk is loaded into memory. Figure 4.4 also shows the structure of the inode (albeit very much simplified). Some of the inode fields point directly to the file data blocks.

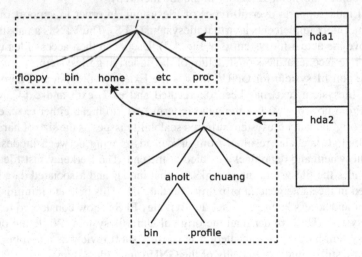

Fig. 4.1 Mounting filesystems

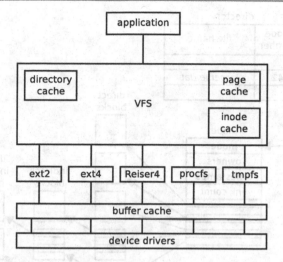

Fig. 4.2 The virtual filesystem

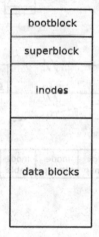

Fig. 4.3 Organisation of the Unix filesystem

For very large files, however, there are insufficient direct pointer fields in the inode. For this reason, some inode fields are used as indirect pointers. An indirect pointer field points to a block of data which contains pointers to other data blocks. These are called single indirect pointers but it is also possible to have double or even triple indirect pointers, see Fig. 4.4.

The ext filesystem is organized into block groups, analogous to cylinder groups in UFS. This is done to reduce external fragmentation and minimize the number of disk seeks when reading a large amount of consecutive data. Each block group contains a superblock, a group descriptor, a block group bitmap, an inode bitmap, followed by the actual data blocks. Backup copies of the superblock are made in every block group but only the first copy of it (which is found at the first block of the file system)

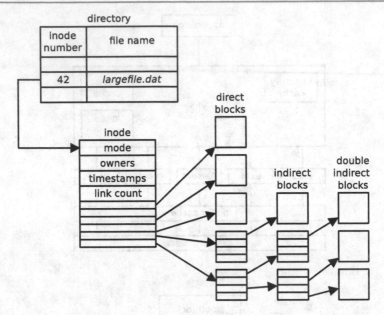

Fig. 4.4 Unix inodes and disk blocks

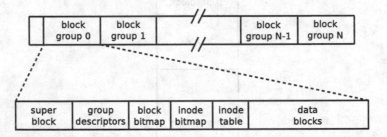

Fig. 4.5 The ext2 filesystem

is used. Figure 4.5 shows the organisation of an ext2 filesystem. We can use a regular file to emulate a filesystem. Create a 64 Mbyte file with the dd command:

```
$ dd if=/dev/zero of=testfs bs=1M count=64
```

Format the file as an ext4 filesystem:

```
$ mkfs.ext4 testfs
mke2fs 1.42.13 (17-May-2015)
Discarding device blocks: done
Creating filesystem with 65536 1k blocks and 16384
inodes
Filesystem UUID: f691a235-cee8-423c-a44e-319c6b13fea4
```

```
Superblock backups stored on blocks:
    8193, 24577, 40961, 57345

Allocating group tables: done
Writing inode tables: done
Creating journal (4096 blocks): done
Writing superblocks and filesystem accounting
information: done
```

Create a mount point and mount *testfs* as a loop device:

```
$ mkdir mnt/
$ sudo mount -o loop testfs mnt/
```

If we look at the top level directory of the filesystem mounted on *mnt*, we see just one directory entry for *lost+found* (which is itself, a directory):

```
$ ls mnt/
lost+found
```

Details of the filesystem can be viewed with the following command-line:

```
$ stat -f mnt/
  File: "mnt/"
    ID: a993df5298bcfba5 Namelen: 255    Type: ext2/ext3
Block size: 1024       Fundamental block size: 1024
Blocks: Total: 59365    Free: 58076    Available: 53490
Inodes: Total: 16384   Free: 16373
```

Unmount the filesystem:

```
$ umount mnt
```

Notice how the values for the filesystem have changed. This is because the content of the *mnt* directory is now on the root filesystem rather than the virtual filesystem in *testfs*:

```
$ stat -f mnt/
  File: "mnt/"
    ID: 87bb65b55155629f Namelen: 255    Type:  ext2/ext3
Block size: 4096       Fundamental block size: 4096
Blocks: Total: 41539898  Free: 4779559    Available:
2663694
Inodes: Total: 10559488   Free: 7900200
```

4.5   Pseudo Filesystems

GNU/Linux supports a number of *pseudo* filesystems. Pseudo filesystems resemble regular filesystems in that they are demountable devices and have a directory based hierarchical structure but they do not map to file storage in the traditional sense. The types of pseudo filesystem are listed below:

- Tmpfs
- Procfs
- Sysfs

Tmpfs is a temporary file storage that uses main memory rather than an external storage device. Files created on a tmpfs are non-persistent across system reboots. Examples of where tmpfs is used are:

/tmp: The */tmp* holds temporary files. It is good practice to use a separate filesystem rather than root itself. While persistent storage could be used for */tmp*, it is common for GNU/Linux systems (embedded or otherwise) to use tmpfs.

/dev/shm: Tmpfs is mounted on the */dev/shm* directory which is used for shared memory. The standard C library, Glibc, expects tmpfs to be mounted on */dev/shm*.

/var: The endurance of solid state devices is not as high as conventional disk drives. For this reason, it is important to keep write operations to the device to a minimum (some embedded systems even mount the root filesystem read-only). The */var* directory, however, *must* be read-write, so for embedded systems that use solid state devices, tmpfs can be used for the */var* directory.

udev: Traditionally, devices files in */dev* were static but it is common for modern GNU/Linux systems to use udev to manage the device files in */dev*. Device files are created dynamically according to udev rules. When udev is used, a tmpfs is mounted on */dev*.

The Proc filesystem (procfs) is an interface to the data structures in kernel. It exposes details about the kernel and running processes to userspace. Typically, procfs is mounted on the */proc* directory and the data structures are grouped into directories similar to the hierarchical structure of a regular filesystem. Procfs provides information about processes and other system information. The concept of sysfs is similar to procfs except that it exposes details of devices to userspace. Sysfs is mounted on */sys*.

A detailed description of procfs and sysfs is beyond the scope of this book but we present a few examples of their use. If we want to know the TCP congestion control algorithm used by the system, we can view the file below:

```
$ cat /proc/sys/net/ipv4/tcp_congestion_control
cubic
```

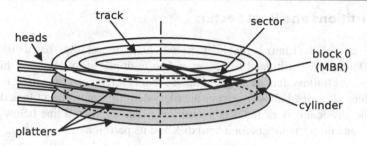

Fig. 4.6 A hard disk

View the MAC address of Ethernet interface eth0:

```
$ cat /sys/class/net/eth0/address
00:1c:23:0c:c7:53
```

Most of the files in procfs are read only but some are writeable. For example, if you need to enable IP packet forwarding, write the value 1 to the file below:

```
$ sudo echo 1 > /proc/sys/net/ipv4/ip_forward
```

4.6 Partitions

In computer systems, disk drives are, typically, used for secondary storage (though solid state devices are growing in popularity). Disk drives are read/write, random access devices and comprise rigid platters rotating about a motor-driven spindle. The platters are coated with a thin layer of magnetic material. Read/write heads float very close the disk surfaces altering the alignment of magnet domains. The magnetic alignment of the domains is used to represent binary data. There are two methods of addressing data on hard disks:

- Logical block addressing (LBA)
- Cylinder-head-sector (CHS)

LBA supersedes the more complex CHS method which references blocks by a cylinder, head and sector three-tuple. Figure 4.6 shows a schematic of the hard disk. Note that each platter has two heads because it has a top and bottom surface. The CHS method of addressing reveals the physical details of disk. Furthermore, CHS only really applies to true hard drives, while solid state drives can report CHS values, they clearly do not reflect the actual geometry of the drive (as we will demonstrate when we create a virtual disk).

4.7 Partitions and Boot Sectors

At a logical level, the Linux kernel interacts with filesystems rather than a disk itself.
Hard disks can be partitioned to accommodate multiple filesystems, in this way
kernel sees each filesystem as a *logical* device that is referenced by a logical index.
Device files (described above) exist in the filesystem for controlling block devices
(either the physical disk or the disk's partitions). The command-line below shows
the major and minor numbers for a hard disk and its partitions:

```
$ stat -c'%N %F %t %T' /dev/sda*
'/dev/sda' block special file 8 0
'/dev/sda1' block special file 8 1
'/dev/sda2' block special file 8 2
'/dev/sda3' block special file 8 3
'/dev/sda5' block special file 8 5
'/dev/sda6' block special file 8 6
```

This gives details of the system hard disk. The major number (in this case 8) references
the device driver used to control the device. The minor number (0–6 in this case)
refers to the instance of the device. The */dev/sda* device, with the minor number 0,
is the physical hard disk. The block devices with non-zero minor numbers (*sda1* to
sda6) are references to the partitions on the disk.

Information about the partitions (as well as code for bootstrapping the operating
system) is kept in a *boot sector*. Boot sectors reside, either on the first block of the
disk (MBR) or in first block of a partition (VBR). See Sect. 2.1 for a more detailed
explanation of MBR and VBR.

For the purpose of this explanation, we will assume we are dealing with a partitioned disk and the boot sector is, therefore, an MBR. The system BIOS makes no
distinction between MBRs and VBRs nor does it understand partitioning. The MBR
may contain a bootstrap program *or* it may contain a boot manager that *chain loads*
bootstraps code in a VBR (on one of the partitions). Table 4.2 describes the structure
of the MBR.

The partition table has space for four partition entries which limits the number of
(primary) partitions to four. Each entry is 16-bits in length, the offsets with the boot
sector are shown in Table 4.3. Table 4.4 shows the structure of a partition table entry.

Table 4.2 Master boot record sector structure

Description	Sector offset		Length (bytes)
	Start	End	
Code area	0	445	446
Master partition table	446	509	64
Boot Record Signature	510	511	2

Table 4.3 Primary partition table

Primary partition table entry	Sector offset	
	Start	End
First	446	461
Second	462	477
Third	478	493
Fourth	494	509

Table 4.4 Partition table entry

Field	Offset	Length	Description
Status	0	1	0x80 bootable
			0x00 non-bootable
Start address	1	3	in CHS form
Partition type	4	1	
End address	5	3	in CHS form
First block of partition	8	4	in LBA form
Partition size	12	4	

In the previous section, we used a regular file to create a *virtual* disk. Here, we use a file to create a virtual disk and demonstrate how the "disk" can be partitioned. Use the command-line below to create a 256 Mbyte file *disk.img*:

```
$ dd if=/dev/zero of=disk.img bs=1024 count=262144
262144+0 records in
262144+0 records out
268435456 bytes (268 MB) copied, 3.96965 s, 67.6 MB/s
```

The fdisk utility is an interactive partition table manipulator. Run fdisk on the virtual disk:

```
$ sudo fdisk -C 8 disk.img
Device contains neither a valid DOS partition table,
nor Sun, SGI or OSF disklabel
Building a new DOS disklabel with disk identifier
0x8f177a4d.
Changes will remain in memory only, until you decide
to write them.
After that, of course, the previous content won't be
recoverable.
```

```
Warning: invalid flag 0x0000 of partition table 4 will
be corrected by w(rite)


Command (m for help):
```

First verify that there are no partitions:

```
Command (m for help): p

Disk disk.img: 0 MB, 0 bytes
255 heads, 63 sectors/track, 8 cylinders, total 0
sectors
Units = sectors of 1 * 512 = 512 bytes
Sector size (logical/physical): 512 bytes / 512 bytes
I/O size (minimum/optimal): 512 bytes / 512 bytes
Disk identifier: 0x8f177a4d

   Device Boot      Start        End      Blocks   Id  System
```

Create a primary partition with the n command:

```
Command (m for help): n
Command action
   e   extended
   p   primary partition (1-4)
p
Partition number (1-4): 1
First sector (1-128519, default 1):
Using default value 1
Last sector, +sectors or +size{K,M,G} (1-128519,
default 128519): 16M
```

Designate this partition type as a FAT32 filesystem (code b):

```
Command (m for help): t
Hex code (type L to list codes): b
Changed system type of partition 1 to b (W95 FAT32)
```

Mark this partition as the boot partition:

```
Command (m for help): a
Partition number (1-4): 1
```

Create another primary partition (64M in size):

```
Command (m for help): n
Command action
   e   extended
   p   primary partition (1-4)
p
Partition number (1-4): 2
First sector (17-128519, default 17):
Using default value 17
Last sector, +sectors or +size{K,M,G} (17-128519,
default 128519): 64M
```

By default, this partition will be a Linux partition. View the newly created partitions:

```
Command (m for help): p

Disk disk.img: 0 MB, 0 bytes
255 heads, 63 sectors/track, 8 cylinders, total 0
sectors
Units = sectors of 1 * 512 = 512 bytes
Sector size (logical/physical): 512 bytes / 512 bytes
I/O size (minimum/optimal): 512 bytes / 512 bytes
Disk identifier: 0x8f177a4d

   Device Boot    Start      End    Blocks   Id  System
disk.img1   *        1       16         8    b   W95 FAT32
disk.img2           17       64        24   83   Linux
```

Write this partition information to the boot sector (MBR):

```
Command (m for help): w
The partition table has been altered!

WARNING: If you have created or modified any DOS 6.x
partitions, please see the fdisk manual page for
additional information.
Syncing disks.
```

Now examine the first block of *disk.img*. Initially *disk.img* contained all zeros, but after running fdisk we can see that the virtual disk has a disk identifier of 0x8f177a4d (note little endian is used):

Table 4.5 Partition entry

Partition	Offet	Fields						
		Status	CHS-start	Type	CHS-end	LBA-start	Size
First	446	80	00 02 00	0b	00 11 00	0000 0001	0000 0010
Second	462	00	00 07 01	83	01 02 02	0000 0011	0000 0030

```
$ od -x -N 16 -j432 -A d -w16 disk.img
0000432 0000 0000 0000 0000 7a4d 8f17 0000 0000
0000448
```

The boot record signature (0x55aa) has been written to the last two bytes of the block:

```
$ od -x -N 16 -j496 -A d -w16 disk.img
0000496 0000 0000 0000 0000 0000 0000 0000 aa55
```

The command-line below shows the area of the MBR for the partition table:

```
$ od -x -N 64 -A d -j446 -w16 disk.img
0000446 0080 0002 000b 0011 0001 0000 0010 0000
0000462 0000 0012 0183 0002 0011 0000 0030 0000
0000478 0000 0000 0000 0000 0000 0000 0000 0000
*
0000510
```

There are two entries, one at offset 446 and one at 462 corresponding to the two partitions we created with fdisk. For clarity, we have presented the partition records above in tabular form in Table 4.5. The status field (byte 0) of the first partition table entry is 0x80, indicating the partition is bootable. Conversely, the second partition is non-bootable because its status field is 0x00. We can also see type fields are 0x0b and 0x83 showing the partitions are for FAT32 and Linux (ext) filesystems, respectively.

We demonstrate how to format these two partitions. We cannot use the filesystem format utilities directly on *disk.img* like we did with *testfs*. Whereas, *testfs* was treated as a filesystem and could be formatted, *disk.img* is emulating an entire disk. It is the partitions within it we wish to format not the file itself. In order to do this we must associate the file with a loopback device. We must also associate the partitions with loopback devices too. For this we use the losetup command. Associate the *disk.img* with a loopback device:

```
$ sudo losetup /dev/loop0 disk.img
```

We can see that */dev/loop0* has been associated with *disk.img*:

```
$ sudo losetup -a
/dev/loop0: [0805]:3944832 (/tmp/disk.img)
```

Also, running fdisk on */dev/loop0* shows partition table we created earlier:

```
$ sudo fdisk -l /dev/loop0

Disk /dev/loop0: 268 MB, 268435456 bytes
255 heads, 63 sectors/track, 32 cylinders, total
524288 sectors
Units = sectors of 1 * 512 = 512 bytes
Sector size (logical/physical): 512 bytes / 512 bytes
I/O size (minimum/optimal): 512 bytes / 512 bytes
Disk identifier: 0x8f177a4d

        Device Boot   Start    End  Blocks  Id  System
/dev/loop0p1            1      16       8    b  W95 FAT32
/dev/loop0p2           17      64      24   83  Linux
```

Next associate the first partition with loopback device */dev/loop1*:

```
$ sudo losetup -o 512 /dev/loop1 /dev/loop0
```

We need to give losetup the start of the partition using the -o (offset) option. The results of fdisk (above) show us that the partition starts at block 1 (the second block) so the offset is 512 bytes. Format the loop1 partition as a MSDOS filesystem (we omit the output from the format command):

```
$ sudo mkdosfs /dev/loop1
```

The filesystem has not been created successfully in the first partition of the disk. Create a mount point and mount the filesystem:

```
$ mkdir msdos
$ sudo mount -t msdos /dev/loop1 msdos
```

Display details of the filesystem with the stat command:

```
$ stat -f msdos
  File: "msdos"
    ID: 70100000000 Namelen: 12      Type: msdos
Block size: 4096         Fundamental block size: 4096
```

```
Blocks: Total: 65467    Free: 65467   Available: 65467
Inodes: Total: 0        Free: 0
```

We repeat the procedure above so that we can format the second partition. Calculate the offset of the partition. Given that fdisk tells us the second partition starts at block 64, the offset is $64 \times 512 = 32768$ bytes. Associate the partition with */dev/loop2*:

```
$ sudo losetup -o 32768 /dev/loop2 /dev/loop0
```

Format the loop2 partition as an ext4 filesystem (we omit the output of the command):

```
$ sudo mkfs.ext4 /dev/loop2
```

Create a mount point and mount the filesystem on it:

```
$ sudo mount /dev/loop2 mnt
```

Check the details of the filesystem:

```
$ stat -f mnt
  File: "mnt"
    ID: 96887f21ce887972 Namelen: 255    Type: ext2/ext3
Block size: 1024         Fundamental block size: 1024
Blocks: Total: 253839  Free: 251777   Available: 238672
Inodes: Total: 65536   Free: 65525
```

4.7.1 Extended Partitions

As we saw with fdisk, when we created a primary partition we only had a choice of four partition numbers. This is because the partition table can only have four entries. Extended partitions were introduced to overcome this limitation. One (and only one) partition in the partition table can be designated an extended partition. Unmount filesystem and delete the loopback devices:

```
$ sudo umount /dev/loop[12]
$ sudo losetup -d /dev/loop[0-2]
```

Run fdisk:

```
$ sudo fdisk disk.img
```

Create a partition:

```
Command (m for help): n
Command action
   e   extended
   p   primary partition (1-4)
```

Select extended partition:

```
e
```

Choose the next available primary partition to be the extended partition (in this case 3):

```
Partition number (1-4): 3
```

Hit return at the next set of prompts to select default values:

```
First sector (65-128519, default 65):
Using default value 65
Last sector, +sectors or +size{K,M,G} (65-128519,
default 128519):
Using default value 128519
```

Display the partition table:

```
Command (m for help): p

Disk disk.img: 0 MB, 0 bytes
255 heads, 63 sectors/track, 8 cylinders, total 0
sectors
Units = sectors of 1 * 512 = 512 bytes
Sector size (logical/physical): 512 bytes / 512 bytes
I/O size (minimum/optimal): 512 bytes / 512 bytes
Disk identifier: 0x8f177a4d

   Device Boot    Start     End  Blocks   Id  System
disk.img1   *         1      16       8    b  W95 FAT32
disk.img2            17      64      24   83  Linux
disk.img3            65  128519   64227+   5  Extended
```

Having set up an extended partition we need to add a partition for a filesystem:

```
Command (m for help): n
Command action
   l   logical (5 or over)
   p   primary partition (1-4)
```

Here we select a logical partition which is located within the extended partition:

```
l
```

Select default values by entering return at the following set of prompts:

```
First sector (66-128519, default 66):
Using default value 66
Last sector, +sectors or +size{K,M,G} (66-128519,
default 128519):
Using default value 128519
```

Verify that the new partition has been created (as a partition for a Linux filesystem):

```
Command (m for help): p

Disk disk.img: 0 MB, 0 bytes
255 heads, 63 sectors/track, 8 cylinders, total 0
sectors
Units = sectors of 1 * 512 = 512 bytes
Sector size (logical/physical): 512 bytes / 512 bytes
I/O size (minimum/optimal): 512 bytes / 512 bytes
Disk identifier: 0x8f177a4d
```

Device Boot		Start	End	Blocks	Id	System
disk.img1	*	1	16	8	b	W95 FAT32
disk.img2		17	64	24	83	Linux
disk.img3		65	128519	64227+	5	Extended
disk.img5		66	128519	64227	83	Linux

Write the partition table to the MBR:

```
Command (m for help): w
The partition table has been altered!

Syncing disks.
```

Table 4.6 Partition entry

Partition	Offset	Fields					
		Status	CHS-start	Type	CHS-end	LBA-start	Size
Extended	478	00	01 03 00	05	fe 3f 07	0000 0041	0001 f5c7
EPBR	33726	00	01 04 00	83	fe 3f 07	0000 0001	0001 f5c6

We can see that a third partition table entry exists in the partition table (offset 478).

```
$ od -x -N 64 -A d -j446 -w16 disk.img
0000446 0080 0002 000b 0011 0001 0000 0010 0000
0000462 0000 0012 0183 0002 0011 0000 0030 0000
0000478 0100 0003 fe05 073f 0041 0000 f5c7 0001
0000494 0000 0000 0000 0000 0000 0000 0000 0000
0000510
```

The extended partition has its own partition table (in the bootblock). The offset of this partition table is $65 \times 512 + 446 = 33726$ bytes. We can see that there is a partition record for the logical partition:

```
$ od -x -N 64 -A d -j33726 -w16 disk.img
0033726 0100 0004 fe83 073f 0001 0000 f5c6 0001
0033742 0000 0000 0000 0000 0000 0000 0000 0000
*
0033790
```

The partition record for the extended partition (third record in the MBR) and the EPBR are shown in Table 4.6.

4.8 Summary

The GNU/Linux file space (like that of Unix) comprises one or more *demountable volumes*, otherwise known as filesystems. A physical hard drive can be divided into a number of filesystems.

The default GNU/Linux filesystem is the extended filesystem (ext2, ext3 or ext4). GNU/Linux, however, supports many different filesystem types which is particularly important for embedded systems. VFS (virtual filesystem) implements a layer of abstraction in order to provide a common interface to physical filesystems, regardless of their type.

We described in detail the anatomy of a hard disk by using a regular file as a virtual disk. We showed how to partition the (virtual) disk so that it could hold multiple filesystems. This enabled us to carry out a detailed analysis of the disk in order to understand its structure. We use these tools in subsequent chapters when we build an embedded system.

Reference

1. Haviland K, Salama B (1987) Unix system programming. Addison-Weseley, Boston

Building an Embedded System (First Pass)

5

In this chapter and the next (Chap. 6) we show how to build embedded GNU/Linux systems. This chapter is a *first pass*. We use various tools to generate the software components so that we can focus on the structure of the system rather than the details. In Chap. 6 (second pass), we cover the topic in greater depth and construct a system from the source code. An operating system (embedded or otherwise) comprises three primary components:

- Bootloader
- Kernel
- Root filesystem.

The filesystem that is mounted on the root directory of the file space is the *root filesystem*. Files required by the operating system in order to function are stored within this directory hierarchy, these include:

- Configuration files
- Start-up/shutdown scripts
- Shared libraries
- System utilities
- User applications

We use the *debootstrap* utility to create the root directory hierarchy. The debootstrap tool creates a base Debian directory hierarchy with the utilities, libraries and configuration files required to run the operating system. The only components that are not generated by debootstrap are the kernel and bootloader.

The Linux kernel itself is stored within the directory hierarchy, though not necessarily on the root filesystem. Typically, the kernel (along with bootloader configuration files) are stored under the */boot* directory. Sometimes a separate filesystem is mounted on */boot*, otherwise */boot* is merely a directory on the root filesystem.

© Springer International Publishing AG, part of Springer Nature 2018
A. Holt and C.-Y. Huang, *Embedded Operating Systems*, Undergraduate Topics in Computer Science, https://doi.org/10.1007/978-3-319-72977-0_5

Instead of running the operating system natively on a physical machine we run it under the control of a virtual machine on the host system upon which it was built. User mode Linux (UML) is a virtualisation technology whereby the Linux kernel is compiled to run as an ELF (executable and linkable format) binary which can be run as a normal user process on a host GNU/Linux system. We use UML to simplify the process of building a kernel. This also obviates the need for a bootloader.

The aim of this chapter is to build a fully functional operating system. We will run it as a virtual machine on a GNU/Linux host. While it will not run natively on an embedded platform, it could with a little extra work. While both of the systems built in this chapter and Chap. 6 are fully functional, they are mainly for educational purposes to illustrate the concepts of embedded operating systems. We do not recommend you use them as production systems.

5.1 Creating the Root Directory Structure

We use the debootstrap tool to generate a base Debian system. The debootstrap tool downloads *.deb* packages from on-line repositories and unpacks them to form a complete system. These repositories are on-line so a host machine will need Internet access. We need to install some utilities for this chapter:

```
$ sudo apt-get install debootstrap uml-utilities
```

Create a directory to work in:

```
$ mkdir ~/deb && cd ~/deb
```

When we run debootstrap it will create a default base system. We can specify additional packages to be included in that base system. We define the packages we wish to include in an environment variable:

```
$ IPKG="udev,locales,resolvconf,rcconf,ssh,\
> net-tools,iputils-ping"
```

Command-line arguments to be passed to debootstrap are defined in an environment variable array:

```
$ OPTS[0]="--variant=minbase"
$ OPTS[1]="--include=${IPKG}"
$ OPTS[2]="--foreign jessie"
$ OPTS[3]="root"
$ OPTS[4]="http://ftp.at.debian.org/debian"
```

The command below creates a Debian Jessie distribution in the directory, *root*:

```
$ sudo debootstrap ${OPTS[*]}
```

The command above may take some time to run depending upon your system and the speed of your Internet connection. We test the system using Docker. First we create an image based upon the debootstrap root directory:

```
$ sudo tar -C root -c . | docker import - deb
```

Set the following options:

```
$ unset OPTS
$ OPTS[0]="--name=deb_init"  # container name
$ OPTS[1]="-d"               # detach
$ OPTS[3]="deb"              # Image name
$ OPTS[4]="/bin/systemd"     # command run in container
```

Run the Docker container:

```
$ docker run ${OPTS[*]}
```

Access the container:

```
$ docker exec -ti deb_init /bin/bash
root@55a0f7363993:/#
```

Note that, root@4a29826c83f8:/# is the container Bash prompt. Check that the init process stared:

```
root@4a29826c83f8:/# ps -e
  PID TTY          TIME CMD
    1 pts/0    00:00:00 systemd
 1146 pts/1    00:00:00 bash
 1157 pts/1    00:00:00 ps
```

We can take the opportunity to set the root password:

```
root@4a29826c83f8:/# passwd
Enter new UNIX password: letmein
Retype new UNIX password: letmein
passwd: password updated successfully
```

Note that, the password program does not echo the password to the screen, thus you will not see the string "letmein". We recommend you use stronger passwords than the examples given in this book. The locales package needs to be reconfigured. this is done by running the command:

```
root@4a29826c83f8:/# dpkg-reconfigure locales
```

Select the appropriate locales from the first menu. In our example, we select:

```
en_GB ISO-8859-1
en_GB.ISO-8859-15 ISO-8859-15
en_GB.UTF-8 UTF-8
```

Hit the <Ok>. From the next menu, we select:

```
en_GB
```

Exit from the container and return to the host:

```
root@4a29826c83f8:/# exit
exit
$
```

5.2 Build the Root Filesystem

As we are running our embedded system as a UML virtual machine, we can create the root filesystem in a virtual partition. We create this partition in a regular file which we format as a filesystem. The command-line below creates a 1024M (regular) file:

```
$ dd if=/dev/zero of=deb_fs seek=1024 count=1 bs=1M
1+0 records in
1+0 records out
```

We format the (*deb_fs*) file as an ext4 filesystem (just as we would for a physical block device):

```
$ mkfs.ext4 -F deb_fs
```

Mount *deb_fs* as a loop device on the root directory:

```
$ sudo mount -o loop deb_fs root
```

Export the root directory structure from the Docker container to the virtual filesystem mount on the *root* directory:

```
$ cd root
$ docker export deb_init | sudo tar -x
```

In order for the virtual machine to access the network, it is necessary to make some configuration changes. Edit the file *root/etc/network/interface* and add the lines shown in Listing 5.1. The IP address, subnet mask and gateway, are selected to work with the Docker virtual bridge, docker0. The operation of the virtual machine's interface to the network bridge is described later on in this chapter.

Listing 5.1 *Configuration of eth0 (/etc/network/interfaces)*

```
auto eth0
iface eth0 inet static
     address 172.17.0.251
     netmask 255.255.255.0
     network 172.17.0.0
     broadcast 172.17.0.255
     gateway 172.17.0.1
```

We will also show how to remotely login to the deb virtual machine using SSH. In order to do this, we need to make a configuration change to the SSH system. Locate the line below in the file *root/etc/ssh/sshd_config*:

```
PermitRootLogin without-password
```

Comment out the line and add a line below, thus:

```
# PermitRootLogin without-password
PermitRootLogin yes
```

This configuration line allows a user to SSH into the virtual machine as superuser. For security reasons we do not advise making this common practice. We do this merely for convenience in order to simplify the exercise. Unmount the filesystem:

```
$ cd ..
$ sudo umount root
```

The filesystem in *deb_fs* now contains the root directory structure.

5.3   Building a User Mode Linux Kernel

In this section we describe how to build a UML kernel. The procedure for building
a UML kernel is virtually the same as building a kernel that runs natively. Create a
directory to work in:

```
$ mkdir ~/uml && cd ~/uml
```

Download the Linux kernel source file:

```
$ mkdir uml && cd uml
$ wget  https://cdn.kernel.org/pub/linux/kernel/v4.x/\
> linux-4.4.tar.gz
```

We use Docker to build the kernel. Create a *Dockerfile* with the contents shown
in Listing 5.2 and create an *entrypoint.sh* shell script with the contents shown in
Listing 5.3.

Listing 5.2 *Contents of* Dockerfile

```
FROM ubuntu:16.04

# install required packages
RUN apt-get -y update && \
    apt-get install -y build-essential \
                       bc \
                       gawk \
                       git-core \
                       libssl-dev \
                       libncurses5-dev \
                       libssl-dev \
                       vim \
                       wget
```

```
WORKDIR /opt
COPY linux-4.4.tar.gz /linux-4.4.tar.gz
COPY entrypoint.sh /entrypoint.sh
CMD /entrypoint.sh
```

Listing 5.3 *Contents of* entrypoint.sh *for building UML*

```
#!/bin/bash

set -e
cd /opt

tar zxvf ../linux-4.4.tar.gz
cd linux-4.4

make defconfig ARCH=um
make menuconfig ARCH=um
make ARCH=um
```

Build the uml Docker image:

```
$ docker build -t uml .
```

Create (and run) a Docker container from the uml image to configure and compile the kernel:

```
$ docker run -v `pwd`/opt:/opt --rm -it uml
```

The container runs the *entrypoint.sh* script. A menu will appear in the terminal window when the script runs the line make menuconfig ARCH=um. By default, the "Enable loadable module support" is turned on. In order to simplify the build, we turn this feature off. Hit the space bar until there is an absence of "*" or "M" between the square brackets "Enable loadable module support" option. Figure 5.1 shows the Enable loadable module support option deselected. Exit from the make makeconfig utility and select "Save".

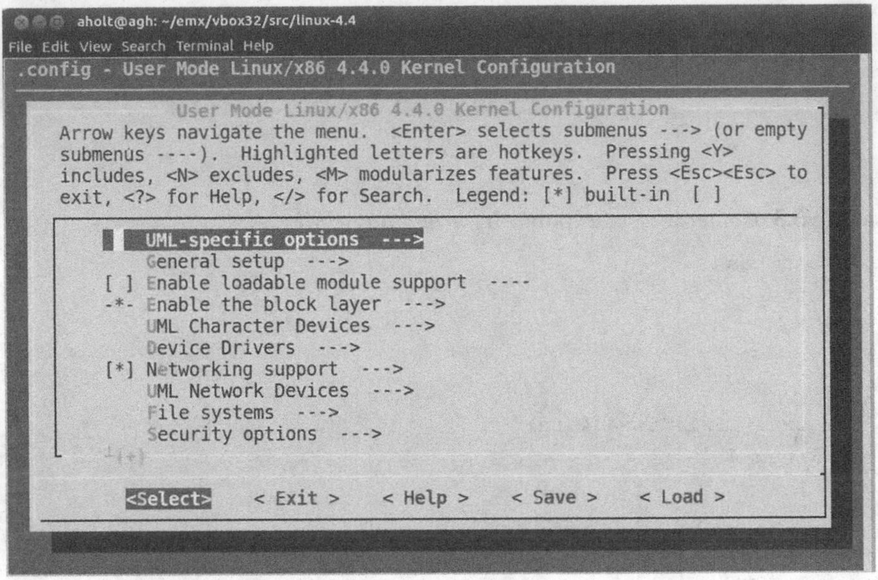

Fig. 5.1 Makeconfig UML

5.4 Running UML

When we compiled the UML kernel, it created an executable file *linux* in the kernel source directory. For convenience, we create a symbolic link to the UML kernel in the file *linux*:

```
$ cd ~/deb
$ ln -s ~/uml/opt/linux4.4/linux linux
```

Listing 5.4 is a launch script for the UML process. Create it in the current directory.

Listing 5.4 *UML Launch Script: uml.sh*

```
#!/bin/bash

FS="deb_fs"
UMID="${FS%%_*}"

OPTS[0]="ubd0=$FS"
OPTS[3]="con=pts con0=fd:0,fd:1"
OPTS[4]="ssl=pts"
```

```
while getopts ":n:s:r:" CMD_LINE_OPTIONS
do
    case $CMD_LINE_OPTIONS in
        r      ) OPTS[0]="ubd0=$OPTARG"
                 UMID="${OPTARG%%_*}"
               ;;
        s      ) OPTS[1]="ubd1=$OPTARG";;
        n      ) OPTS[2]="eth0=tuntap,$OPTARG,,";;
        *      ) echo "Unimplemented option";;
    esac
done

OPTS[5]="umid=${UMID}"

./linux ${OPTS[*]}
```

Make the launch script executable:

```
$ chmod +x uml.sh
```

Here, we describe how to configure the deb virtual machine for networking. Figure 5.2 shows the host system with the UML deb system running as a virtual machine. The host has an Ethernet interface eth0. This is a physical interface connected to an external Ethernet network (which in turn is connected to the wider Internet). In our case, the IP details of eth0 were configured through the dynamic host control protocol (DHCP).

The deb virtual machine also has an eth0 interface which we can bind to a virtual network interface uth0 on the host. In addition, a virtual bridge (ubridge) needs to be configured on the host and uth0 is attached to it. We could configure a new bridge, however, the Docker system uses one for its containers. We can, therefore, use the existing docker0 bridge. The command below, shows the Docker bridge:

```
$ brctl show
bridge name   bridge id STP enabled  interfaces
docker0       8000.024240a47331  no          veth86ed30b
```

Figure 5.2 also shows the network address translation (NAT) between the bridge and the host's eth0 interface.

Create a virtual Ethernet interface and bring it up:

```
$ sudo tunctl -u aholt -t uth0
$ sudo ifconfig uth0 0.0.0.0 promisc up
```

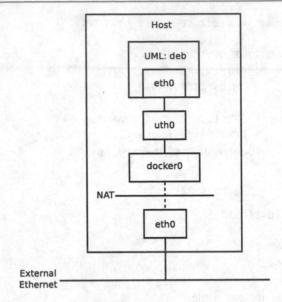

Fig. 5.2 UML networking architecture

Attach interface uth0 to the docker0 bridge:

```
$ brctl addif docker0 uth0
```

Verify that the virtual interface is attached to docker0:

```
$ brctl show docker0
bridge name   bridge id STP enabled   interfaces
docker0       8000.024240a47331   no            uth0
                                          veth86ed30b
```

We are now in a position to launch a virtual machine running the deb operating with
networking capabilities:

```
$ ./uml.sh -n uth0
```

A sequence of kernel debug messages are displayed on the screen as the system boots
up. When the init process starts it runs gettys on the consoles and serial lines. At the
end of the boot process you should see some lines like those below:

```
Virtual console 6 assigned device '/dev/pts/14'
Virtual console 1 assigned device '/dev/pts/15'
```

```
Virtual console 2 assigned device '/dev/pts/16'
Virtual console 3 assigned device '/dev/pts/17'
Virtual console 4 assigned device '/dev/pts/18'
Virtual console 5 assigned device '/dev/pts/19'
```

This shows us which pseudo terminals on the host are attached to the consoles and serial lines of the host. From a new terminal window, login to console 1 with using the minicom tool:

```
$ sudo minicom -D /dev/pts/15
```

We are presented with a login prompt (it may be necessary to hit a key to wake up the getty). Login as "root" and use the password we set earlier:

```
Debian GNU/Linux 8 localhost tty6

localhost login: root
Password: letmein
```

Note that, the string "letmein" is not echoed to the screen. The message of the day is displayed followed by a command-line prompt:

```
Linux localhost 4.4.0 #1 Fri Jul 28 19:26:22 UTC 2017
x86_64

The programs included with the Debian GNU/Linux system
are free software; the exact distribution terms for
each program are described in the individual files in
/usr/share/doc/*/copyright.

Debian GNU/Linux comes with ABSOLUTELY NO WARRANTY, to
the extent permitted by applicable law.
root@localhost:~#
```

Verify the Ethernet interface has an IP address:

```
root@localhost:~# ifconfig eth0
eth0 Link encap:Ethernet  HWaddr c2:1f:c6:16:0f:08
     inet addr:172.17.0.251  Bcast:172.17.0.255
Mask:255.255.255.0
     UP BROADCAST RUNNING MULTICAST  MTU:1500  Metric:1
     RX packets:132 errors:0 dropped:4 overruns:0 frame:0
     TX packets:7 errors:0 dropped:0 overruns:0 carrier:0
     collisions:0 txqueuelen:1000
```

```
       RX bytes:25215 (24.6 KiB)  TX bytes:574 (574.0 B)
       Interrupt:5
```

Test the network functionality from the host with the ping utility. This shows that the virtual machine can communicate with one of Google's DNS servers on the Internet:

```
root@localhost:~# ping -c 4 8.8.8.8
PING 8.8.8.8 (8.8.8.8) 56(84) bytes of data.
64 bytes from 8.8.8.8: icmp_seq=1 ttl=53 time=22.5 ms
64 bytes from 8.8.8.8: icmp_seq=2 ttl=53 time=23.4 ms
64 bytes from 8.8.8.8: icmp_seq=3 ttl=53 time=23.5 ms
64 bytes from 8.8.8.8: icmp_seq=4 ttl=53 time=23.4 ms

--- 8.8.8.8 ping statistics ---
4 packets transmitted, 4 received, 0% packet loss, time
3006ms
rtt min/avg/max/mdev = 22.572/23.274/23.575/0.421 ms
```

The host machine is connected with the virtual machine through the Docker bridge as this is the Docker container we ran earlier to test the deb system. As the virtual machine is running an SSH server (which we configured above) we should be able to remotely login to it from both the host machine and the Docker container. Attach to the deb_init container:

```
$ docker exec -it deb_init /bin/bash
```

SSH to the virtual machine:

```
root@8c1805504d64:/# ssh root@172.17.0.251
root@172.17.0.5's password: letmein  # not displayed
  :

  :
root@localhost:~#
```

Verify that we are logged in via a pseudo terminal as well as over the network (from the Docker container with IP address 172.17.0.2):

```
root@localhost:~# who
root      tty2         2017-07-31 09:49
root      pts/0        2017-07-31 11:01 (172.17.0.2)
```

5.5 Summary

In this chapter we described how to build an embedded system using the debootstrap utility and a UML kernel. With debootstrap, we built the root filesystem with all the shared libraries, utilities, start-up scripts and configuration files required by the operating system. We used a UML kernel so that we could run the system as a virtual machine on a host GNU/Linux system. The UML kernel obviates the need for a bootloader because we can start the kernel like any other user process. We also showed how the system could be networked.

Building an Embedded System (Second Pass)

6

In the previous chapter we showed how to build an embedded system which ran in a virtual machine. We will refer to this system as the "deb" system to distinguish it from the embedded system described in this chapter.

The root filesystem for the deb system was generated using the debootstrap utility. This created the root directory structure and installed the necessary libraries, binary utilities, scripts and configuration files required for the system. To complete the root filesystem, we only needed to make minor amendments to some of the configuration files. We built a UML kernel so that we could run deb as a virtual machine on a host machine. This obviated the need for a bootloader. Debootstrap and UML greatly simplified the task of building the system.

In this chapter, we examine the components of an embedded GNU/Linux system in more detail. We show how to build a system without the aid of automated tools such as debootstrap. Further, we will build a system that runs natively on an embedded platform. It is a minimal system that we build, but it is fully functional. We divided the build process into several stages which are outlined below:

Administration: Create configuration files and start-up scripts.

Glibc: Much of the software of a Unix (and Unix-like) system is written in the C language. Common operations, such as input/output, memory management, string manipulation, for example, are not part of the language itself. Rather, they are provided through a standard library (either statically linked in at compile time or dynamically at run time). Glibc is a standard C library for GNU/Linux.

Ncurses: Ncurses provides a library of screen-handling functions for writing GUI-like applications in text-based terminals. Ncurses functions form a wrapper around terminal control-codes so that applications can be developed in a terminal independent way.

© Springer International Publishing AG, part of Springer Nature 2018
A. Holt and C.-Y. Huang, *Embedded Operating Systems*, Undergraduate
Topics in Computer Science, https://doi.org/10.1007/978-3-319-72977-0_6

Busybox: Most of the utilities in the deb system were from part of the coreutils
and util-linux packages. These packages are designed for general purpose operating systems. For systems with limited resources (such as embedded systems)
coreutils and util-linux can take up a lot of disk space. The Busybox package
provides common GNU/Linux utilities but is designed specifically for embedded
environments. Busybox is highly customisable, enabling cut down versions of the
original Unix utilities to be compiled into a single binary image.

Sysvinit: The kernel starts the init process at boot-time. The init process, in turn,
starts all the services (daemon processes) on the system as well as *getty* processes
which wait for logins on console and tty devices. We compile the init utility from
the Sysvinit package.

The kernel: In the previous chapter we compiled a UML kernel, that is, a kernel
that can be run as a regular process. In this chapter we shall build a system to run
on an actual embedded platform. Therefore, we need to build and install a kernel
that runs natively.

The bootloader: The bootloader is responsible for loading the kernel into memory
and passing control to it. We use Extlinux which is a derivative of Syslinux. Unlike
Syslinux, which can only boot a kernel from a FAT filesystem, Extlinux can boot
the system from an ext filesystem.

The target system for this operating system build is a Soekris net4521 [1]. The
net4521 has an i486 133 MHz processor, 64 MB SDRAM, two Ethernet ports, one
Serial port and compact flash (CF) socket (see Fig. 6.1). It should be possible to
run this system on any Intel based platform. Only the kernel compilation procedure
requires special attention as the configuration options would need to be congruent
to the target platform's hardware.

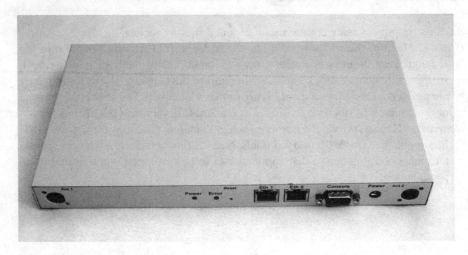

Fig. 6.1 Soekris net4521

6.1 Preliminaries

Create directories to work in:

```
$ mkdir -p ~/emx/{root,src}
$ cd ~/emx/src
```

Now we download the component parts of the operating system software described above. Get the source code for the Linux kernel:

```
$ wget https://cdn.kernel.org/pub/linux/kernel/v3.x/\
> linux-3.16.tar.gz
```

Fetch Glibc:

```
$ wget http://ftp.gnu.org/pub/gnu/glibc/\
> glibc-2.19.tar.gz
```

Download Ncurses:

```
$ wget http://ftp.gnu.org/pub/gnu/ncurses/\
> ncurses-5.9.tar.gz
```

Download Busybox:

```
$ wget https://busybox.net/downloads/\
> busybox-1.26.2.tar.bz2
```

6.2 Administrative Files

In this section we create configuration files and start-up/shutdown scripts. Change directory:

```
$ cd ~/emx/
```

Create the target system's root directory structure, thus:

```
$ mkdir -p root/{boot,etc,proc,root,sys,var}
```

The kernel and bootloader stages are stored in the *root/boot* directory. The *root/root* directory is the home directory for the root (superuser) account. The *root/proc* and *root/sys* directories are mounted points for the procfs and sysfs filesystems, respectively (see Sect. 4.5). The target's configuration files reside, primarily, in the *root/etc* directory. Create the *root/etc/profile.d* subdirectory:

```
$ mkdir -p root/etc/profile.d
```

Create *root/etc/network* directory and the subdirectories that will contain scripts for configuring the network interface:

```
$ mkdir -p root/etc/network/\
> {if-down.d,if-post-down.d,if-pre-up.d,if-up.d}
```

The *motd* file contains a message of the day that is displayed when the user logs in and *issue* contains a message that is displayed prior to login. We create empty versions of these files:

```
$ touch root/etc/{motd,issue}
```

It is left to the reader to populate the *motd* and *issue* files.

Password authentication requires two files, namely, *passwd* and *group*. Most modern GNU/Linux systems include a shadow password file (*shadow*) for extra security. For convenience, we will not use a shadow password file. The *passwd* file contains the valid user accounts for the system. There is one line of configuration per user. Each user must belong to a group. Groups are defined in the *group* file. We only need to define an account for the Superuser along with a corresponding group. Create a files *root/etc/passwd* and *root/etc/group* with the contents shown in Listings 6.1 and 6.2, respectively.

Listing 6.1 *Contents of /etc/passwd*

```
root::0:0:Superuser:/root:/bin/ash
```

Listing 6.2 *Contents of /etc/group*

```
root:!:0:
```

Glibc library is able to access database information from various sources using the name service switch (NSS). The *nsswitch.conf* file specifies the sources of these databases. Create the *root/etc/nsswitch.conf* with contents shown in Listing 6.3.

Listing 6.3 *Contents of /etc/nsswitch.conf*

```
passwd:             files
group:              files
shadow:             files
hosts:              files dns
networks:           files
protocols:          fIles
services:           files
```

Create the file *root/etc/profile* with contents shown in Listing 6.4.

Listing 6.4 *Contents of /etc/profile*

```
#!/bin/sh

for i in /etc/profile.d/*
do
        . $i
done
```

In *root/etc/profile.d*, create the file: *env*, with the contents shown in Listing 6.5.

Listing 6.5 *Contents of /etc/env*

```
export PS1='\u@\h:\w\$ '
```

The contents of the file *root/etc/hostname* are shown in Listing 6.6. This file determines the name of the system when it boots up. Create the file as specified.

Listing 6.6 *Contents of /etc/hostname*

```
emx
```

Create the *root/etc/inittab* with contents shown in Listing 6.7.

Listing 6.7 *Contents of /etc/inittab*

```
# $Id: inittab,v 1.91 2002/01/25 13:35:21 miquels Exp $

id:2:initdefault:

si::sysinit:/etc/init.d/rcS

~:S:wait:/sbin/sulogin

l0:0:wait:/etc/init.d/rc 0
l1:1:wait:/etc/init.d/rc 1
l2:2:wait:/etc/init.d/rc 2
l3:3:wait:/etc/init.d/rc 3
l4:4:wait:/etc/init.d/rc 4
l5:5:wait:/etc/init.d/rc 5
l6:6:wait:/etc/init.d/rc 6
z6:6:respawn:/sbin/sulogin

ca:12345:ctrlaltdel:/sbin/shutdown -t1 -a -r now

pf::powerwait:/etc/init.d/powerfail start
pn::powerfailnow:/etc/init.d/powerfail now
po::powerokwait:/etc/init.d/powerfail stop

1:2345:respawn:/sbin/getty 38400 tty1
2:23:respawn:/sbin/getty 38400 tty2
3:23:respawn:/sbin/getty 38400 tty3
4:23:respawn:/sbin/getty 38400 tty4
5:23:respawn:/sbin/getty 38400 tty5
6:23:respawn:/sbin/getty 38400 tty6

T0:23:respawn:/sbin/getty -L ttyS0 9600 vt100
T1:23:respawn:/sbin/getty -L ttyS1 9600 vt100
```

The *fstab* file specifies the mounted filesystems. Listing 6.8 shows the contents of *root/etc/fstab*. During the course of its operation, GNU/Linux writes data to files in the */var* directory. The problem is that our root filesystem will be on a solid state device, namely, a compact flash card. Solid state devices have a much shorter *endurance* than conventional hard disks. If */var* is on the root filesystem, then continual writes to the directory will shorten the lifetime of the compact flash. It is not uncommon for the embedded devices to mount the root filesystem read-only in order to protect the solid state device. Clearly this causes a problem when the system needs to write to */var*. To overcome this problem, a tmpfs is mounted on */var*.

Listing 6.8 *Contents of /etc/fstab*

```
proc /proc proc defaults 0 0
sysfs /sys sysfs defaults 0 0
tmpfs /dev/shm tmpfs defaults 0 0
tmpfs /tmp tmpfs defaults 0 0
tmpfs /var tmpfs defaults 0 0
```

The system expects a directory structure below */var* but, data is not persistent in a temporary filesystem. For this reason we have to create the directory structure at boot-time. This is done in the *bootmisc* start-up script shown in Listing B.4 below. It does this by untarring a file which contains the underlying directory structure once the temporary filesystem has been mounted on */var*. Create a (temporary) *var* directory and subdirectories:

```
$ mkdir -p var/{,log/,run/,run/network/,tmp/}
```

Create a tar file of the directory structure and copy it to the *root* directory:

```
$ tar cf var.tar var/
$ cp var.tar root/
```

The temporary *var* directory can now be cleaned up:

```
$ rm -rf var/
```

The *services* file specifies the mapping between Internet services and transport (UDP and TCP) port numbers. The most convenient way to generate this file is copy it from the host:

```
$ cp /etc/services root/etc/
```

Listing 6.9 shows the content of *root/etc/network/interfaces* which specifies the configuration of the network interfaces (lo and eth0). We configure eth0 to have an IP address in the range of the Docker bridge, docker0.

Listing 6.9 *Content of /etc/network/interfaces*

```
auto lo
iface lo inet loopback

auto eth0
iface eth0 inet static
```

```
address 172.17.0.252
netmask 255.255.255.0
network 172.17.0.0
broadcast 172.17.0.255
gateway 172.17.0.1
```

While we use static IP details for this example, we may need to use DHCP. First, create the directory: *root/usr/share/udhcpc*:

```
$ mkdir -p root/usr/share/udhcpc
```

Create a file *default.script* in the directory *root/etc/usr/share/udhcpc/* with the content shown in Listing A.1. The file can be found in the cloned git repository. For convenience, the reader can copy the file *~/emxbook/emx/chapter6/section6.2/default.script* into *root/etc/usr/share/udhcpc/*.

6.3 Start-up Scripts

We need to write a number of start-up (and shutdown) scripts that are run by init. The start-up/shutdown scripts are located in the *root/etc/init.d* directory. These scripts are run according to the runlevel the system is in. For each runlevel there is an *rc* directory which contains symbolic links to the start-up/shutdown scripts relevant to that runlevel. Create the *init.d* and rc (sub)directories:

```
$ mkdir root/etc/init.d
$ mkdir root/etc/rc{S.d,0.d,1.d,2.d,3.d,4.d,5.d,6.d}
```

For brevity, the code listings for all the start-up/shutdown scripts are in Appendix B. A list of the start-up/shutdown scripts are given below:

rcS: The rcS script is the boot-time system initialisation script which runs other start-up scripts. Listing B.1 shows the rcS script. The line below from the *root/etc/inittab* file (Listing 6.7) causes this script to run:

```
si::sysinit:/etc/init.d/rcS
```

rc: The rc scripts runs the */etc/inittab* file (Listing 6.7) and defines the system states under which the rc scripts are run. For example, the line below runs the rc script with the argument "2" for runlevel 2:

```
12:2:wait:/etc/init.d/rc 2
```

Listing B.2 shows the rc script. The script runs a sequence of other scripts which can either start-up or shutdown a service.

mountall: The mountall script (in its start-up form) mounts all the filesystem list-ed in */etc/fstab*. For this system, these are the tmpfs filesystem and the procfs filesystem. It also re-mounts the root filesystem read-write (whereas, up to this mount it was mounted read-only). In its shutdown form, mountall umounts all the filesystems. See Listing B.3.

bootmisc: The bootmisc script. See Listing B.4.

hostname: Configure the hostname of the system. See Listing B.5.

telnet: Starts/stops the Telnet daemon. See Listing B.9.

ntp: Starts/stops the network time protocol (NTP). See Listing B.10.

syslogd: Starts/stops the syslog daemon. See Listing B.7.

klogd: Start/stops the kernel log daemon. See Listing B.8.

halt: Initiates a shutdown of the system. See Listing B.11.

reboot: Initiates a reboot of the system. See Listing B.12.

These files are in the git repository that accompanies this book and can be found in the directory *~/emxbook/emx/chapter6/files/init.d*. Make the start-up scripts executable:

```
$ chmod +x ~/emx/root/etc/init.d/*
```

We create symbolic links to the start-up/shutdown scripts in the rc directories. Links to start-up scripts begin with an "S" while links to shutdown scripts begin with a "K". Create symbolic links in rcS.d:

```
$ cd ~/emx/root/etc/rcS.d
$ ln -s ../init.d/mountall S35mountall
$ ln -s ../init.d/bootmisc S37bootmisc
$ ln -s ../init.d/hostname S40hostname
$ ln -s ../init.d/network S40network
```

Create symbolic links in rc0.d:

```
$ cd ../rc0.d
$ ln -s ../init.d/klogd K89klogd
$ ln -s ../init.d/syslogd K90syslogd
$ ln -s ../init.d/network K95network
$ ln -s ../init.d/mountall K97mountall
$ ln -s ../init.d/halt S99halt
```

Create symbolic links in rc2.d:

```
$ cd ../rc2.d
$ ln -s ../init.d/syslogd S10syslogd
$ ln -s ../init.d/klogd S11klogd
```

Create symbolic links in rc6.d:

```
$ cd ../rc6.d
$ ln -s ../init.d/klogd K89klogd
$ ln -s ../init.d/syslogd K90syslogd
$ ln -s ../init.d/network K95network
$ ln -s ../init.d/mountall K97mountall
$ ln -s ../init.d/reboot S99reboot
```

6.4 Devices (/dev)

Special devices files are located in the */dev* directory. The deb system built in the previous chapter included a utility called udev which created the devices at boot-time. Here we need to create the device files manually at install time. First create the *dev* directory and some sub-directories under it:

```
$ cd ~/emx/root
$ mkdir -p dev/{,misc,shm,ubd}
```

We need to create a number of character devices in *root/dev*. Create the console using mknod:

```
$ cd dev
$ sudo mknod -m 660 console c 5 1
```

Create the serial lines:

```
$ sudo mknod -m 660 ttyS0 c 4 64
$ sudo mknod -m 660 ttyS1 c 4 65
```

Create a number of tty devices:

```
$ sudo mknod -m 660 tty0 c 4 0
$ sudo mknod -m 660 tty1 c 4 1
$ sudo mknod -m 660 tty2 c 4 2
```

```
$ sudo mknod -m 660 tty3 c 4 3
$ sudo mknod -m 660 tty4 c 4 4
$ sudo mknod -m 660 tty5 c 4 5
$ sudo mknod -m 660 tty6 c 4 6
```

The ptmx device is used to create a master and slave pair for a pseudo terminal. Two file descriptors are returned to any process that open /dev/ptmx. One descriptor is for a master pseudo terminal and the other is for the slave. Create the ptmx device:

```
$ sudo mknod ptmx c 5 2
```

Create real timne clock device:

```
$ sudo mknod -m 660 misc/rtc c 10 135
```

The null device acts as a data sink for write operations and the zero device returns 0×00 characters when read. While null and zero are treated as "devices" they do not correspond to actual physical hardware. Create the *null* and *zero* devices:

```
$ sudo mknod null c 1 3
$ sudo mknod zero c 1 5
```

Create the block devices for the hard disk, which in this case, is a compact flash card:

```
$ sudo mknod --mode=660 hda b 3 0
$ sudo mknod --mode=660 hda1 b 3 1
$ sudo mknod --mode=660 hda2 b 3 2
```

The *hda* device is the disk itself, while the *hda1* and *hda2* devices are partitions of the disk (for filesystems). While we intend to build this system to run natively on an embedded platform, we will test it on a UML virtual machine first. For this reason we need to create devices for the UML filesystems (though these will be redundant when the system runs on the actual embedded devices):

```
$ sudo mknod --mode 660 ubd/0 b 0 98
$ sudo mknod --mode 660 ubd/1 b 1 98
```

6.5 Compile the Operating System Software

In order to avoid cross-compiling 32-bit software on a 64-bit machine, we set up a 32-bit virtual machine. The virtual machine platform that we use is VirtualBox, but we use Vagrant set it up:

```
$ vagrant init bento/debian-8.6-i386
```

For convenience, we need to mount directories on our host system to directories within our virtual machine environment. Open up the file *Vagrantfile* in a text editor and locate the line:

```
config.vm.box = "bento/debian-8.6-i386"
```

Immediately after the line above, add the following lines:

```
config.vm.synced_folder "root/", "/home/vagrant/root"
config.vm.synced_folder "src/", "/home/vagrant/src"
```

Exit from the text editor and save the file. Bring up the vagrant virtual machine:

```
$ vagrant up --provider virtualbox
```

Check the virtual machine is running:

```
$ vagrant global-status
id        name     provider    state    directory
-----------------------------------------------------------
90be763  default  virtualbox  running  /home/aholt/emx
```

SSH into the virtual machine:

```
$ vagrant ssh
```

The prompt `vagrant@debian-8:~$` indicates that the commands issued here are on the virtual machine. Install the *gawk* and libncurses5-dev packages:

```
vagrant@debian-8:~$ sudo apt-get -y install \
> gawk libncurses5-dev git
```

6.5.1 Glibc

In this section we show how to build the GNU C library, Glibc. Glibc is by far the most difficult component of system to build. Once Glibc have been successfully compiled, the other components are relatively straight forward. Create *tools* and *build* directories:

```
vagrant@debian-8:~$ mkdir tools build
```

Glibc requires the headers files from Linux kernel. We downloaded version 3.16 of the kernel in Sect. 6.1. Untar the Linux headers and change directory:

```
vagrant@debian-8:~$ tar zxvf src/linux-3.16.tar.gz
vagrant@debian-8:~$ cd linux-3.16/
```

We do not need to compile the whole kernel at this stage, we just need to build the headers for Glibc:

```
vagrant@debian-8:~$ make headers_check
vagrant@debian-8:~$ make \
> INSTALL_HDR_PATH=../tools headers_install
```

Extract the Glibc source files:

```
vagrant@debian-8:~$ cd  # return to HOME directory
vagrant@debian-8:~$ tar zxvf src/glibc-2.19.tar.gz
```

It is important to note Glibc cannot be built in its own source directory. We therefore use a separate *build* directory (which we created above) for this purpose:

```
vagrant@debian-8:~$ cd build
```

Set the CFLAGS environment variable:

```
vagrant@debian-8:~$ export \
> CFLAGS="-march=i486 -O3 -fno-stack-protector"
```

Glibc, like many of the components we compile, requires a number of configuration options. For convenience and brevity we use an environment variable array to define them:

```
vagrant@debian-8:~$ OPTS[0]="--prefix=/usr"
vagrant@debian-8:~$ OPTS[1]=\
> "--with-headers=../tools/include"
vagrant@debian-8:~$ OPTS[2]="--host=i486-pc-linux-gnu"
vagrant@debian-8:~$ OPTS[3]="--disable-profile"
vagrant@debian-8:~$ OPTS[4]="--disable-sanity-checks"
vagrant@debian-8:~$ OPTS[5]="--without-gd"
vagrant@debian-8:~$ OPTS[6]="--without-selinux"
```

Configure Glibc:

```
vagrant@debian-8:~$ ../glibc-2.19/configure ${OPTS[*]}
```

Compile the software:

```
vagrant@debian-8:~$ make
```

Install the Glibc library:

```
vagrant@debian-8:~$ make install \
> install_root=/home/vagrant/root
```

Create the *ld.so.conf* file in the *root/etc* directory with the contents shown in Listing 6.10.

Listing 6.10 *Contents of /etc/ld.so.conf*

```
/lib
/usr/lib
/usr/local/lib
```

If disk space is at a premium, we can reduce the size of some files by removing the symbols from object files. We can even remove some files altogether. Use the strip utility to remove the symbols from object files:

```
vagrant@debian-8:~$ strip root/lib/*.so
```

Remove the include directory:

```
vagrant@debian-8:~$ rm -rf root/usr/include
```

Use the sequence of commands below to remove redundant files:

```
vagrant@debian-8:~$ cd ~/root/usr/share/locale
vagrant@debian-8:~$ ls | grep -v locale.alias | \
> xargs rm -rf
vagrant@debian-8:~$ cd ~/root/usr/share/i18n/charmaps
vagrant@debian-8:~$ ls  | grep -v -E  -w '8859|UTF' | \
> xargs rm
vagrant@debian-8:~$ cd ~/root/usr/share/i18n/locales
vagrant@debian-8:~$ ls  | \
> grep -v -E -w 'en_GB|en_US|POSIX' | sudo xargs rm
```

6.5.2 Ncurses

Ncurses is a library of screen-handling functions. Applications, such as vi, make use of Ncurses. Extract the source files for Ncurses:

```
vagrant@debian-8:~$ cd
vagrant@debian-8:~$ tar zxvf src/ncurses-5.9.tar.gz
```

Make the Ncurses directory the working directory:

```
vagrant@debian-8:~$ cd ncurses-5.9
```

Set the CFLAGS environment variable:

```
vagrant@debian-8:~$ export CFLAGS="-march=i486 -O3"
```

Set the configuration options:

```
vagrant@debian-8:~$ unset OPTS
vagrant@debian-8:~$ OPTS[0]="--prefix=$HOME/root"
vagrant@debian-8:~$ OPTS[1]="--disable-database"
vagrant@debian-8:~$ OPTS[2]=\
> "--with-fallbacks=linux,vt100,xterm,rxvt"
vagrant@debian-8:~$ OPTS[3]="--with-shared"
vagrant@debian-8:~$ OPTS[4]="--without-normal"
vagrant@debian-8:~$ OPTS[5]="--without-debug"
vagrant@debian-8:~$ OPTS[6]="--without-ada"
vagrant@debian-8:~$ OPTS[7]="--without-progs"
vagrant@debian-8:~$ OPTS[8]="--without-cxx"
vagrant@debian-8:~$ OPTS[9]="--libdir=$HOME/root/lib"
```

Configure Ncurses:

```
vagrant@debian-8:~$ ./configure ${OPTS[*]}
```

Compile and install the Ncurses library:

```
$ make && make install
```

We complete the Ncurses install by running some optimisation commands. Remove
the symbols from the library file:

```
vagrant@debian-8:~$ strip root/lib/libncurses.so.5.9
```

Delete the manual pages and include files:

```
vagrant@debian-8:~$ rm -rf root/{man,include}
```

6.5.3 Busybox

Extract the Busybox source from the tar file and change to the resultant directory:

```
vagrant@debian-8:~$ cd    # change to HOME directory
vagrant@debian-8:~$ tar jxvf src/busybox-1.26.2.tar.bz2
vagrant@debian-8:~$ cd busybox-1.26.2
```

We need to make a small modification to the default Busybox configuration. Busybox
provides its own version of init. We found that there was a problem with the Busybox
version of init running on the Soekris. For this reason we used the standard init from
the Sysvinit package (described below). We, therefore, need to configure Busybox to
omit compiling init. Run the menu based configuration utility using the command-
line below:

```
vagrant@debian-8:~$ make menuconfig
```

Go to the Init Utilities section and disable the init option. This is done by selecting
the option and hitting the space bar until there is an absence of "*" or "M" between
the square brackets:

```
[ ] init
```

Now exit and save the configuration. Set compiler and library flags:

```
vagrant@debian-8:~$ export CFLAGS="-march=i486"
vagrant@debian-8:~$ export LDFLAGS="-L ~/root/lib"
```

Compile and install Busybox:

```
vagrant@debian-8:~$ make
vagrant@debian-8:~$ make CONFIG_PREFIX=~/root install
```

At this point we can carry out a test of the system by using a chroot jail:

```
vagrant@debian-8:~$ cd
vagrant@debian-8:~$ sudo chroot root /bin/sh -i
/ #
```

Verify the / directory of the emx system:

```
/ # ls -l /
total 44
drwxrwxr-x    2 1000     1000      4096 Jun 22 11:43 bin
drwxrwxr-x    2 1000     1000      4096 May  8 12:50 boot
drwxrwxr-x    5 root     root       380 Jul 31 15:12 dev
drwxrwxr-x   13 1000     1000      4096 Jul 31 15:32 etc
drwxrwxr-x    2 1000     1000      4096 Jun 21 09:29 lib
lrwxrwxrwx    1 1000     1000        11 Jun 22 08:33 linuxrc
-> bin/busybox
dr-xr-xr-x  247 root     root         0 Jul 31 15:12 proc
drwxrwxr-x    2 1000     1000      4096 Jul 31 15:26 root
drwxrwxr-x    2 1000     1000      4096 Jun 22 12:21 sbin
dr-xr-xr-x   13 root     root         0 Jul 31 15:12 sys
drwxrwxr-x    7 1000     1000      4096 Jun 21 08:11 usr
drwxrwxr-x    5 1000     1000      4096 Jul 31 15:12 var
-rw-rw-r--    1 1000     1000     10240 May  8 12:50 var.tar
```

Exit the chroot jail:

```
/ # exit
vagrant@debian-8:~$
```

6.5.4 Sysvinit

We install the init utility from Sysvinit package rather than using the Busybox version.
Ensure you have disabled the init configuration option in the Busybox section above.
Clone the git respository for Sysvinit:

```
vagrant@debian-8:~$ cd
vagrant@debian-8:~$ git clone \
> https://github.com/Distrotech/sysvinit.git
```

Set compiler flags (if not already set):

```
vagrant@debian-8:~$ export CFLAGS="-march=i486"
```

There is no need for a configuration process, we can simply compile it:

```
vagrant@debian-8:~$ cd sysvinit1/src
vagrant@debian-8:~$ make init
```

We can install the init program simply by copying it to the appropriate directory:

```
vagrant@debian-8:~$ cp init ~/root/sbin
```

The telinit utility is used to instruct init to perform certain actions. We "create" telinit
simply by creating a symbolic link to init itself:

```
vagrant@debian-8:~$ cd ~/root/sbin
vagrant@debian-8:~$ ln -s init telinit
```

We have now finished working on the virtual machine and can return to the host
(note the change of prompt):

```
vagrant@debian-8:~$ exit
$
```

We can test the system using Docker to ensure init is working and starts up the
respective services. We build a Docker container as a *lightweight* virtual machine
using our emx root filesystem. Import the root directory structure for the emx system
into a docker image (ensure you are in the *emx* directory):

```
$ sudo tar -C root -c . | docker import - emx
```

Check the image has been created:

```
$ docker images emx
REPOSITORY   TAG      IMAGE ID      CREATED         SIZE
emx          latest  5ce31c4fa633  2 minutes ago   29.7MB
```

Now we create a Docker container based upon the emx image. Set the following environment variables:

```
$ unset OPTS
$ OPTS[0]="--name=emx_init"      # container name
$ OPTS[1]="-d"                   # detach
$ OPTS[2]="emx"                  # Image name
$ OPTS[3]="/sbin/init"           # command to run
```

Run Docker to create the container:

```
$ docker run ${OPTS[*]}
```

Check that the emx_init Docker container is running using the docker ps command. For brevity, we use the -filter flag to control the output fields. We define the filter's template in the environment variable, thus:

```
$ FORMAT="table {{.ID}}:\t{{.Status}}:\t{{.Names}}"
```

Note that, the only reason we do this is to control the width of the output for the book. You may omit the -filter flag from the command below. Check the emx_init container is running:

```
$ docker ps --format="${FORMAT}"
CONTAINER ID:       STATUS:            NAMES
b006aa3d12ce:       Up 10 minutes:     emx_init
8c1805504d64:       Up 27 hours:       deb_init
```

Notice that, in our case, the deb_init container is still running. Access the emx_init container:

```
$ docker exec -ti emx_init /bin/sh
/ #
```

Check the init process is running and that the start-up scripts were executed:

```
/ # ps
PID   USER      TIME    COMMAND
   1 root       0:00 init [2]
  36 root       0:00 /sbin/syslogd
  40 root       0:00 /sbin/getty 38400 tty1
  41 root       0:00 /sbin/getty 38400 tty2
  42 root       0:00 /sbin/getty 38400 tty3
  43 root       0:00 /sbin/getty 38400 tty4
  44 root       0:00 /sbin/getty 38400 tty5
  45 root       0:00 /sbin/getty 38400 tty6
  46 root       0:00 /sbin/getty -L ttyS0 9600 vt100
  47 root       0:00 /sbin/getty -L ttyS1 9600 vt100
  48 root       0:00 /bin/sh
  55 root       0:00 ps
```

Check Ethernet interface has been configured:

```
/ # ifconfig eth0
eth0 Link encap:Ethernet  HWaddr 02:42:AC:11:00:03
     inet addr:172.17.0.3  Bcast:0.0.0.0  Mask:255.255.0.0
     UP BROADCAST RUNNING MULTICAST  MTU:1500  Metric:1
     RX packets:731 errors:0 dropped:0 overruns:0 frame:0
     TX packets:3 errors:0 dropped:0 overruns:0 carrier:0
     collisions:0 txqueuelen:0
     RX bytes:33706 (32.9 KiB)  TX bytes:1026 (1.0 KiB)
```

Verify that the network is functioning by pinging the deb container (which should still be running):

```
/ # ping -c 4 172.17.0.2
PING 172.17.0.2 (172.17.0.2): 56 data bytes
64 bytes from 172.17.0.2: seq=0 ttl=64 time=0.311 ms
64 bytes from 172.17.0.2: seq=1 ttl=64 time=0.249 ms
64 bytes from 172.17.0.2: seq=2 ttl=64 time=0.277 ms
64 bytes from 172.17.0.2: seq=3 ttl=64 time=0.249 ms

--- 172.17.0.2 ping statistics ---
4 packets transmitted, 4 packets received, 0% packet loss
round-trip min/avg/max = 0.249/0.271/0.311 ms
```

We leave it up to the reader to verify that the Internet can be accessed from this container. Take the opportunity to set the root password:

```
/ # passwd
Changing password for root
New password: letmein
Bad password: too weak
Retype password: letmein
passwd: password for root changed by root
```

Once again, we remind the reader that the password is not actually echoed to the screen. Furthermore, we ignore the warning that the password is too weak. Exit from the container:

```
~ # exit
$
```

6.6 Test Under UML

We aim to run this system natively on a physical CPU. We still have some work to do but we should be able to run the system in its current form under UML. Create a 256 MB file for a root virtual filesystem (ensure you are in the *emx* directory):

```
$ dd if=/dev/zero of=emx_fs seek=256 count=1 bs=1M
1+0 records in
1+0 records out
```

Format *emx_fs* as an ext4 filesystem (for brevity we omit the output of mkfs.ext4):

```
$ mkfs.ext4 -F emx_fs
```

Mount the filesystem as a loopback device:

```
$ sudo mount -o loop emx_fs root
```

Note that the mount point for the *emx_fs* filesystem is the directory *root* which was the directory in which we created the file structure for the emx system. The mount operation does not affect the contents of / directory. The *emx_fs* filesystem is merely *overlayed* on the current filesystem at the mount point, *root/*. When we list the content of *root* we see just the one file that exists in the / directory of the *emx_fs* filesystem, namely, *lost+found*.

```
$ ls root/
lost+found
```

Export the root filesystem from the emx_init container to the *emx_fs* filesystem:

```
$ cd root/
$ docker export emx_init | sudo tar -x
$ cd ..
$ sudo umount root
```

Now we need to build a UML kernel, create a directory to work in:

```
$ mkdir ~/emx/uml && cd ~/emx/uml
```

Copy the kernel into the current directory:

```
$ cp ../src/linux-3.16.tar.gz .
```

Listings 6.11 and 6.12 show the contents for the *Dockerfile* and the script *entrypoint.sh*, respectively. Create these files in the current directory (*~/emx/uml*):

Listing 6.11 *Contents of Dockerfile*

```
FROM ubuntu:12.04

# install required packages
RUN apt-get -y update && \
    apt-get install -y build-essential \
                       bc \
                       gawk \
                       git-core \
                       gcc-multilib \
                       g++-multilib \
                       libssl-dev \
                       libncurses-dev \
                       libc6-dev-i386 \
                       vim

WORKDIR /opt
COPY linux-3.16.tar.gz /linux-3.16.tar.gz
COPY entrypoint.sh /entrypoint.sh
ENTRYPOINT /entrypoint.sh
```

Listing 6.12 *Contents of entrypoint.sh*

```
#!/bin/bash

set -e

cd /opt

tar zxf ../linux-3.16.tar.gz
cd linux-3.16

make defconfig ARCH=um
make menuconfig ARCH=um
make ARCH=um
```

Build the image:

```
$ docker build -t uml32 .
```

Set the options for the docker run command:

```
$ unset OPTS
$ OPTS[0]="--name=uml_make"          # container name
$ OPTS[1]="-v `pwd`/opt:/opt"        # mount vol
$ OPTS[2]="-it"                      # interactive
$ OPTS[3]="--rm"                     # remove on termination
$ OPTS[4]="uml32"                    # Image name
```

Build the UML kernel by running uml_make container:

```
$ docker run ${OPTS[*]}
```

Copy the *uml.sh* script in Listing 5.4 into the current directory. Create a link to the UML kernel:

```
$ ln -s uml/linux-3.16/linux linux
```

Run the emx system as a UML virtual machiine:

```
$ ./uml.sh -r emx_fs -n uth0
```

As the system boots, the pseudo termials that are mapped to the TTYs are displayed:

```
Virtual console 6 assigned device '/dev/pts/13'
Serial line 0 assigned device '/dev/pts/18'
Serial line 1 assigned device '/dev/pts/19'
Virtual console 5 assigned device '/dev/pts/21'
Virtual console 4 assigned device '/dev/pts/22'
Virtual console 3 assigned device '/dev/pts/23'
Virtual console 2 assigned device '/dev/pts/24'
Virtual console 1 assigned device '/dev/pts/25'
```

Open a new terminal window and choose one of the PTYs and login to the system:

```
$ sudo minicom -D /dev/pts/23
```

Login as root using the password set earlier:

```
emx login: root
Password: letmein    # not echoed to screen
~ #
```

We leave it to the reader to check that the services are running and the network interface is operational. Shutdown the UML virtual machine:

```
~ # halt
INIT: Switching to runlevel: 0
INIT: Sending processes the TERM signal
Stopping klogd: klogd stopped sucessfully.
Stopping syslogd: syslogd stopped sucessfully.
Take down network interfaces: done.
umount: can't unmount /dev: Device or resource busy
EXT4-fs (ubda): re-mounted. Opts: (null)
Halting... reboot: System halted
$
```

6.7   Running the System Natively

Having tested that the system (so far) runs successfully in a Docker container and on a UML virtual machine, we complete the final steps so that we can run it natively on a i486 Soekris device. The Soekris uses a compact flash as its hard drive. We summerise the steps for preparing the compact flash below:

- Create the partition table (fdisk)
- Format the partition as an ext4 filesystem
- Install the root directory structure
- Install the kernel
- Install the bookloader

First we must connect the compact flash to the host system. For this we need a compact flash reader. These are usually connected to the host system via a USB. Before connecting the compact flash reader (with the compact flash inserted) to the host check the */proc/partitions* file. On our system the content of the file looks like this (it is likely the output will be different on your system):

```
$ cat /proc/partitions
major minor  #blocks   name

   8       0  156290904 sda
   8       1     102400 sda1
   8       2   39062500 sda2
   8       3          1 sda3
   8       5  113282316 sda5
   8       6    3839503 sda6
```

Connect the compact flash reader to the host computer and repeat the command above. You should see some additional lines (how many, will depend upon the number of partitions already configured on the compact flash card):

```
   8      16      62720 sdb
   8      17      62713 sdb1
```

The output above tells us that the compact flash device is */dev/sdb* and it has a single partition (*/dev/sdb1*). The operating system may be configured to automatically mount filesystems when the drive is connected to the host. If this is the case, then unmount the filesystems:

```
$ sudo umount /dev/sdb1
```

First we create a partition table using fdisk:

```
$ sudo fdisk /dev/sdb
```

Check for any existing partition table entries:

```
Command (m for help): p

Disk /dev/sdb: 64 MB, 64225280 bytes
2 heads, 62 sectors/track, 1011 cylinders, total 125440
sectors
Units = sectors of 1 * 512 = 512 bytes
Sector size (logical/physical): 512 bytes / 512 bytes
I/O size (minimum/optimal): 512 bytes / 512 bytes
Disk identifier: 0x00000000

   Device Boot     Start        End     Blocks  Id  System
```

Create a partition:

```
Command (m for help): n
Command action
   e   extended
   p   primary partition (1-4)
```

Select a primary partition

```
p
```

Select 1 as the partition number and hit return at each subsequent prompt:

```
Partition number (1-4): 1
First sector (2048-125439, default 2048):
Using default value 2048
Last sector, +sectors or +size{K,M,G} (2048-125439,
default 125439):
Using default value 125439
```

Make the partition bootable and select 1 when prompted for the partition:

```
Command (m for help): a
Partition number (1-4): 1
```

Check the details of the partition created:

```
Command (m for help): p

Disk /dev/sdb: 64 MB, 64225280 bytes
2 heads, 62 sectors/track, 1011 cylinders, total
125440 sectors
Units = sectors of 1 * 512 = 512 bytes
Sector size (logical/physical): 512 bytes / 512 bytes
I/O size (minimum/optimal): 512 bytes / 512 bytes
Disk identifier: 0x00000000

   Device Boot     Start        End    Blocks  Id System
/dev/sdb1     *      2048     125439     61696  83 Linux
```

Write the partition table to the disk:

```
Command (m for help): w
The partition table has been altered!

Calling ioctl() to re-read partition table.
Syncing disks.
```

Format the partition:

```
$ sudo mkfs.ext4 /dev/sdb1
```

Mount the compact flash drive on the root directory:

```
$ sudo mount /dev/sdb1 root/
$ cd root/
```

Export the root directory structure from the emx_init container into the */dev/sdb1* filesystem:

```
$ docker export emx_init | sudo tar -x
```

Unmount */dev/sdb1*:

```
$ cd ..
$ sudo umount root
```

We need to make a small modification to the *inittab* file. The Soekris does not have physical hardware for the tty [1–6] devices. Lines in the *root/etc/inittab* file like the one below, will cause init to respawn getty processes too quickly:

```
2:23:respawn:/sbin/getty 38400 tty2
```

As a result, the message below will be displayed on the console periodically:

```
INIT: Id "2" respawning too fast: disabled for 5 minutes
```

In order to prevent this rapid respawning (and the subsequent messages), comment out the lines in the *root/etc/inittab* file that respawn gettys on tty [1–6], see below:

```
#1:2345:respawn:/sbin/getty 38400 tty1
#2:23:respawn:/sbin/getty 38400 tty2
#3:23:respawn:/sbin/getty 38400 tty3
#4:23:respawn:/sbin/getty 38400 tty4
#5:23:respawn:/sbin/getty 38400 tty5
#6:23:respawn:/sbin/getty 38400 tty6
```

Obviously, you can omit the steps above if you are using a platform with physical hardware for these tty devices.

6.7.1 Compiling the Kernel

This subsection describes how to build a kernel for an x86 processor. It is similar to building a UML kernel but we need to generate a configuration file for the target host. The kernel comprises many options. Unfortunately, an explanation of all the options required for even a modest embedded system is outside the scope of this book. See [2] for a general description of Linux kernel options. The options file for the Soekris net4521 can be found in the git repository that accompanies this book (see Sect. 3.1). Create a directory to work in:

```
$ mkdir ~/soekris && cd ~/soekris
```

Copy the file in (*~/emxbook/emx/chapter6/config.soekris*) to this directory. Create the *Dockerfile* with the contents shown in Listing 6.13. We create a Docker image, soekris, based upon the uml32:latest image that we created in Sect. 6.6 for building a UML kernel. This way, the 3.16 kernel source code will reside in the resultant soekris image.

Listing 6.13 *Contents of Dockerfile*

```
FROM uml32:latest

WORKDIR /opt
COPY config.soekris /config.soekris
COPY entrypoint_soekris.sh /entrypoint_soekris.sh
ENTRYPOINT /entrypoint_soekris.sh
```

We pass a new entrypoint script to the soekris image. The contents of *entrypoint_script.sh* is shown in Listing 6.14.

Listing 6.14 *entrypoint_soekris.sh*

```
#!/bin/bash

set -e
cd /opt

tar zxf ../linux-3.16.tar.gz
cd linux-3.16
cp /config.soekris .config

make menuconfig
make
```

Build the soekris container:

```
$ docker build -t soekris .
```

Set the `docker` run options:

```
$ unset OPTS
$ OPTS[0]="--name=soekris_make"   # container name
$ OPTS[1]="-v `pwd`/opt:/opt"     # mount vol
$ OPTS[2]="-it"                   # interactive
$ OPTS[3]="--rm"                  # remove on termination
$ OPTS[4]="soekris"               # Image name
```

Configure and compile the kernel:

```
$ docker run ${OPTS[*]}
```

Install the kernel onto the root filesystem

```
$ cp System.map ~/soekris/boot/System.map-3.16
$ cp .config ~/soekris/boot/config-3.16
$ cp arch/i386/boot/bzImage ~/soekris/boot/bzImage-3.16
```

6.7.2 The Bootloader

Syslinux is a collection of lightweight bootloaders for various filesystem types. The
Syslinux bootloader itself is for MS-DOS filesystems only. While the root filesystem
is ext4, we could create an MS-DOS *boot* filesystem which holds the Syslinux
bootloader files. In order to reduce the complexity of having two filesystems, we use
the Extlinux version of the bootloader that works with ext filesystems. We use Docker
to compile the software. Create the Dockerfile with content shown in Listing 6.15.
Then create the *entrypoint.sh* script shown in Listing 6.16.

Listing 6.15 *Contents of Dockerfile*

```
FROM i386/debian

# install required packages
RUN apt-get -y update && \
    apt-get install -y build-essential \
                       bc \
                       e2fslibs-dev \
                       gawk \
                       libncurses5-dev \
                       libssl-dev \
                       nasm \
                       vim \
                       uuid-dev \
                       wget

WORKDIR /opt
COPY syslinux-6.03.tar.gz /syslinux-6.03.tar.gz
COPY entrypoint.sh /entrypoint.sh
ENTRYPOINT /entrypoint.sh
```

Listing 6.16 *Contents of entrypoint.sh*

```
#!/bin/bash
```

```
set -e
cd /opt

tar zxf ../syslinux-6.03.tar.gz
cd syslinux-6.03/
make bios installer
```

Build the image:

```
$ docker build -t syslinux .
```

```
$ unset OPTS
$ OPTS[0]="--name=syslinux_make" # container name
$ OPTS[1]="-v 'pwd'/opt:/opt" # mount vol
$ OPTS[2]="--rm"  # remove on termination
$ OPTS[3]="-it"  # Interactive terminal
$ OPTS[4]="syslinux"  # Image name
```

Build EXTLINUX by running the container:

```
$ docker run ${OPTS[*]}
```

Install the bootloader:

```
$ ./extlinux --install ~/emx/root/boot/extlinux
```

The bootloader needs a configuration file: *~/emx/root/boot/extlinux/extlinux.conf*.
Create this file with the content shown in Listing 6.17.

Listing 6.17 *Contents of /boot/extlinux/extlinux.conf*

```
SERIAL 0 19200
DEFAULT linux
LABEL linux
SAY Now booting the kernel from SYSLINUX...
KERNEL /boot/bzImage-2.6.35.13
    APPEND ro root=/dev/hda1 console=ttyS0,19200n8
TIMEOUT 30
PROMPT 1
```

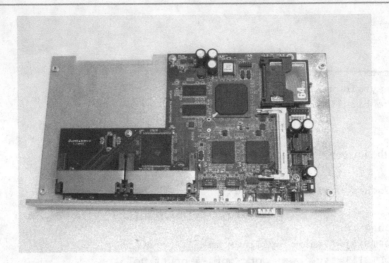

Fig. 6.2 Soekris motherboard showing compact flash card

The system is now complete and we unmount the CF drive:

```
$ cd ~/emx
$ sudo umount root
```

6.7.3   Booting the System

We are now ready to boot the system from the compact flash card. The compact flash socket is located inside the Soekris so it is necessary to remove the cover (Fig. 6.2). Plug the compact flash card into the compact flash socket (then replace the cover). We then need to connect up the Soekris to a host and the local Ethernet network as shown in Fig. 6.3. In our case, the host machine was a laptop (running GNU/Linux).

The serial port of the Soekris is connected to the serial port of the host. The init program is configured to run a getty on the Soekris unit's serial 0 (ttyS0). If we run a terminal emulator on the host we can gain access to Soekris through a serial link. As both the host and the Soekris are data terminal equipment (DTE) the serial cable needs to be a *null modem*. Table 6.1 shows the pin-out configuration for both 25- and 9-pin connectors. Rather than making a null modem cable it would be just as easy to purchase one from an electrical retailer. As with many modern laptops, ours did not have a serial port. We, therefore, had to use one of the USB ports with a USB-serial converter cable.

Power up the Soekris and run the command below:

```
$ mount -D /dev/ttyUSB0
```

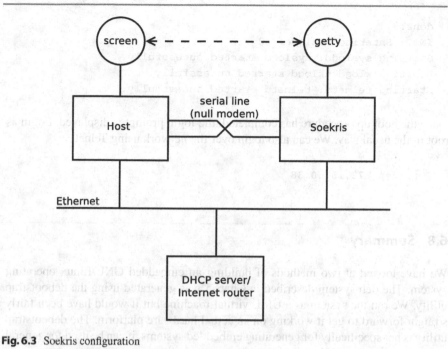

Fig. 6.3 Soekris configuration

Table 6.1 Null modem

Signal	From		To		Description
	25-pin	9-pin	25-pin	9-pin	
Grd	1	–	1	–	Ground
Tx	2	3	3	2	Transmit
Rx	3	2	2	3	Receive
RTS	4	7	5	8	Request to send
CTS	5	8	4	7	Clear to send
Sig Grd	7	5	7	5	Signal ground
DSR	6	6	20	4	Data set ready
DCD	8	1	20	4	Data carrier ready
DTR	20	4	6/8	6/1	Data terminal ready

Statements from the boot procedure will be displayed on the screen. Once the kernel has booted, it runs the init process, which in turn starts the systems services:

```
udhcpc (v1.19.3) started
Sending discover...
Sending select for 172.16.50.38...
Lease of 172.16.50.38 obtained, lease time 86400
```

```
done.
INIT: Entering runlevel: 2
Starting syslogd: syslogd started sucessfully.
Starting klogd: klogd started sucessfully.
Starting telnetd: telnetd started sucessfully.
```

Once the boot up procedure has completed, the login prompt is displayed. Login as root in the usual way. We can also login over the network using Telnet:

```
$ telnet 172.16.50.38
```

6.8 Summary

We have looked at two methods of building an embedded GNU/Linux operating system. The deb system described in Chap. 5 was generated using the debootstrap utility. We ran the system as a UML virtual machine but it would have been fairly straight forward to get it working on an actual hardware platform. The debootstrap utility is not specifically for generating embedded systems, it can be used for general computing systems such as desktops, laptops and servers.

We built the emx system manually, compiling all the source code and creating all the necessary subdirectories, system and device files. The emx system was tested with UML but we took the system a stage further and ran it on a Soekris embedded platform.

While the deb system is quite small it is large for an embedded system. It does, however, offer the flexibility of adding packages post-installation through the Debian package management utility (Apt).

The emx system, in contrast, is much smaller, consequently, it has fewer features and is quite limited in its usefulness. Unlike the deb system, utilities can be added to the system but this cannot be done dynamically while the system is running due to the lack of a package manager. New software has to be compiled from source then installed on the root filesystem. This can be done direct to the compact flash card (or whatever device is being used as a hard drive) provided it is mounted on the host system. Compiling software from source can be fraught with problems. Most packages are dependent upon software libraries from other packages (which in turn can be dependent upon other libraries). Compiling a particular package can, therefore, involve having to build many dependencies. Package managers like Apt resolve dependency issues automatically. Fortunately, many GNU/Linux utilities are supported by Busybox albeit they are usually lightweight versions of the originals.

The emx system's compact size is not necessarily an advantage over deb. We were able to fit the emx root filesystem on a 64 MB compact flash. However, these days, it is difficult to buy solid state drives this small. At the time of writing this book a browse through the Amazon web site revealed the smallest compact flash card was 4 GB, which is more than enough to accommodate even the deb root filesystem.

References

1. Soekris Engineering. http://sockris.com/products.html. Accessed 14 May 2013
2. Kroah-Hartman G (2009) Linux kernel in a Nutshell. O'Reilly Media, Sebastopol

Compiler Toolchains

7

Most software is written in a high level programming language such as C, Java, Perl or Python. High-level languages comprise machine independent instructions which cannot be directly executed by the processor. High-level language instructions, therefore, must be translated into machine level (or machine dependent) instructions.

High level languages are often categorised as either compiled or interpreted. A compiled language is translated from source code to object code prior to execution using a program called a *compiler*. The compiler produces an executable file from a file (or files) containing the source code.

With interpreted languages, the source code is translated and executed line by line. Interpreted languages are more convenient than compiled languages. They are more portable because code can be executed on any machine architecture that has the interpreter. However, the execution of interpreted code tends to be slower, because (high-level) instructions must be translated (into low level instructions) each time they are executed.

This distinction between compiled and interpreted languages has blurred somewhat with the arrival of languages such as Java and Python. These languages are compiled into a *bytecode* which is then executed by an interpreter.

The compiler translates high-level instructions into machine code in a number of stages. Compilers, therefore, are rarely a single program, but rather a collection of programs. This collection of programs is called a *toolchain* because they are each run as a chain of commands, each passing its output to the next program in the chain. The final program in the chain will generate the object code in a file. The main stages (programs) in a compiler toolchain are:

- Preprocessor
- Code generator
- Assembler
- Linker

© Springer International Publishing AG, part of Springer Nature 2018
A. Holt and C.-Y. Huang, *Embedded Operating Systems*, Undergraduate
Topics in Computer Science, https://doi.org/10.1007/978-3-319-72977-0_7

As this book is about embedded operating systems we are interested in a particular type of toolchain, namely a *cross toolchain*. Given that embedded systems are limited in resources (typically) it is impractical to compile source code for an embedded system on the system itself. For this reason, source code compilation is performed on a host machine which may have different processor architecture to the embedded system. A cross compiler toolchain is a toolchain that runs on a host system of a particular architecture but builds software for a target system of a different architecture. In this chapter we discuss compiler toolchains. We restrict our discussion to the GNU compiler collection (GCC) as it is the established toolchain for the GNU/Linux system (though it is not exclusive to GNU/Linux). In the last part of the chapter we show how to build a cross compiler toolchain.

7.1 GCC

GCC (GNU compiler collection) is a set of compilers. GCC was originally just a C compiler (and was called the GNU C compiler) but it now can compile other languages, such as C++, Fortran, Pascal and Java. GCC is the primary compiler for GNU/Linux. The use of GCC is not confined to open source projects, it is also used for commercial and proprietary development.

In the following example we show how to compile the ubiquitous "hello world" program. The C source code is shown in Listing 7.1.

Listing 7.1 *hello.c*

```
#include <stdio.h>

int main ()
{
    printf("hello world\n");
    return 0;
}
```

Compile the source *hello.c* with GCC:

```
$ gcc -Wall -o hello hello.c
```

This produces a binary file *hello* which contains the binary executable code. We can run the resultant program, thus:

```
$ ./hello
hello world
%
```

In the example above, GCC has performed all the "compilation" stages but it is possible to terminate the procedure at intermediate stages using GCC's options. In the subsections below, we discuss the individual compilation stages.

7.1.1 The Preprocessor

C, like a number of languages, requires a preprocessing phase. The purpose of the preprocessor is to remove the features of the source code that improves its readability. The GCC preprocessor is cpp. The preprocessor performs the following tasks:

- Removes comments (replacing them with a single space).
- Expands any macro definitions.
- Removes any line breaks unless they are in literals.
- Replaces #include lines with the respective file contents.
- Re-assemble lines the programmer has split up for clarity.
- Tokenizes keywords and builds table of symbols which might be used for code generation.

We demonstrate the role of the preprocessor in the next example. Listing 7.2 shows a simple C program *incr.c*.

Listing 7.2 *Content of incr.c*

```
/* incr.c
    Preprocessor example
*/

#include "incr.h"

main() {

    int x = 0; /* declare an integer x */

    /* increment the value 2 and assigns to x */
    x = \
        incr(2);

}
```

The #include directive tells the preprocessor to load the content of the specified file at the point the directive appears in the original source file. The text delimited by /* and */ are comments. In this case, the include file is *incr.h* and is shown in Listing 7.3.

Listing 7.3 *Content of incr.h*

```
/* incr.h
   Defines increment macro
*/

#define incr(n) n + 1
```

The #define directive specifies a macro, in this case called incr. The macro takes
an argument (just like a function call) to which 1 is added. Also, the assignment of
x is split over two lines. This is unnecessary but we want to demonstrate how the
preprocessor reassembles lines. Two file names are passed as arguments to cpp. The
first file is the infile and contains the initial C source code to be preprocessed (in this
case *incr.c*). Any files specified in the #include directive of the infile will also be
processed. The second file is the outfile which cpp writes the resultant preprocessed
code to. Run cpp, thus:

```
$ cpp incr.c incr.cpp
```

The command-line above produces an output file *incr.cpp*, the content of which is
shown in Listing 7.4.

Listing 7.4 *Content of incr.cpp*

```
# 1 "incr.c"
# 1 "<built-in>"
# 1 "<command-line>"
# 1 "incr.c"
# 1 "incr.h" 1
# 2 "incr.c" 2


main() {

    int x = 0;

    x = 2 + 1;

}
```

We can see that the cpp has performed a number of preprocessing tasks. Firstly, the
code from *incr.h* has been included. The comments have been removed and replaced

with a single space. The assignment statement of x, which was split over two lines, has been re-assembled into one. Finally, the macro statement incr(2) has been replaced with the statement: x = 2 + 1.

7.1.2 Optimisation

The purpose of the optimisation step is to try and maximise or minimise some attribute of the executable code, for example:

- Size of the binary image.
- Execution speed.
- Memory usage.
- Energy consumption (this is of particular relevance embedded systems).

In addition, the optimisation process may reduce the actual execution time and memory use of the compilation itself. Optimisation is an optional step in the compilation of the code. GCC supports a number of levels of optimisation which can be specified through command-line options. See Table 7.1 for a description of GCC optimisation levels.

Here we present a simple example of code optimisation. We compare optimisation level 1 with level 0 (no optimisation) using code in Listing 7.5.

Table 7.1 GCC optimisation options

Level	Option	Comment
0	-O0	No optimisation. This is the same as omitting the -O option
1	-O1 or -O	Performs optimisation functions that do not require any speed/space trade-off. The size of the binary image should be smaller and its execution speed faster compared to the -O0 level. Furthermore the compilation can be shorter
2	-O2	Performs additional optimisation (over that of -O1) that do not require any speed/space trade-off. Executions speed should be faster without increasing the size of the image. Compilation times could be slower
2.5	-Os	Performs optimisation aimed at reducing the size of the generated code. In some cases this can also improve performance because there is less code to execute
3	-O3	The aim of this level of optimisation is to increase execution speed. It does this at the cost of increasing the binary image size. In some cases the increase in code can have the effect of reducing performance
3	-Ofast	Performs optimisation that disregards standards compliance

Listing 7.5 *Optimisation example: content of opt.c*

```
#include <stdio.h>

#define N 100000

int main()
{
    long i, j, k = 0;

    for(i = 0; i < N; i++)
        for(j = 0; j < N; j++)
            k += (i - j);


    printf("k = %ld\n", k); /* k = 0 */
}
```

Compile the *opt.c* for optimisation levels 0 and 1:

```
$ gcc -O0 -o opt0 opt.c
$ gcc -O1 -o opt1 opt.c
```

Run the executable for optimisation level 0:

```
$ time ./opt0
k = 0

real    0m31.729s
user    0m31.702s
sys 0m0.000s
```

Now run the executable for level 1:

```
$ time ./opt1
k = 0

real    0m9.080s
user    0m9.065s
sys 0m0.004s
```

We can see that optimised code executes in about a third of the time compared to the none optimised code. We leave to the reader to test the code execution time for optimisation levels 2 and 3.

7.1.3 The Assembler

Assembly language is a low-level programming language where machine language operations are represented by mnemonics. There is (usually) a one-to-one correspondence between numerical machine language operations and assembly language mnemonic instructions. The GCC code generator converts high-level language instructions to assembly code. This code is passed to the assembler which translates the assembly language instructions in machine code.

The C source code in Listing 7.6 declares a variable x and assigns the value 42 to it. The function main returns the value of x.

Listing 7.6 *Content of file decl.c*

```
int main() {
    int x = 42;
    return x;
}
```

Compile *decl.c* but stop the process at the assembler stage (-S):

```
$ gcc -Wall -S decl.c
```

This produces assembly code in the file *decl.s* shown in Listing 7.7.

Listing 7.7 *Content of file decl.s*

```
    .file   "decl.c"
    .text
    .globl main
    .type   main, @function
main:
    pushl   %ebp
    movl    %esp, %ebp
    subl    $16, %esp
    movl    $42, -4(%ebp)
    movl    -4(%ebp), %eax
    leave
    ret
    .size   main, .-main
```

```
.ident    "GCC: (Ubuntu 4.4.3-4ubuntu5.1) 4.4.3"
.section    .note.GNU-stack,"",@progbits
```

Run the assembler to translate the assembly language instructions into object code (*decl.o*):

```
$ as -o decl.o decl.s
```

We still need to perform the linker stage on the object code, so we call gcc to complete the compilation process:

```
$ gcc -o decl decl.o
```

Run the binary executable and check the return code:

```
$ ./decl
$ echo $?
42
```

7.1.4 The Linker

Large programs are normally broken into multiple source files for convenience. These source files are combined and compiled together to form a single executable. For very large software development projects, it is convenient to compile into separate object code blocks. While object code comprises machine dependent instructions, it cannot be executed. The toolchain has to perform the final stage and *link* the separate object code blocks into a single executable. The advantage of organising the software into separate object code blocks is that if a change is made to one part of the (source) code, only the object code block that is affected needs to be compiled rather than the entire code. Object code files have the suffix `.o`. The linker can also link object code from libraries. There are two varieties of library:

- Static libraries (suffix `.a`).
- Dynamic shared libraries (suffix `.so`).

In the previous section we ran the assembler to translate assembly instructions into machine dependent code. We had to run the linker (gcc with the `-o` switch) to generate the final executable binary code. This is because each object code module's address starts at zero. The linker combines these various object code modules and performs code *relocation*. If we compare *decl.o* and *decl*, we see that *decl.o* contains relocatable code whereas *decl* contains executable code:

```
$ file decl.o decl
decl.o: ELF 32-bit LSB relocatable, Intel 80386, version
1 (SYSV), not stripped
decl:   ELF 32-bit LSB executable, Intel 80386, version
1 (SYSV), dynamically linked (uses shared libs), for
GNU/Linux 2.6.15, not stripped
```

The function of the linker is demonstrated in the example below:

```
$ gcc -c -o mean.o mean.c
```

The source code for *mean.c* is shown in Listing 7.8. The command above generates a file *mean.o* which contains the compiled (but not linked) object code.

Listing 7.8 *Content of file mean.c*

```
double mean(double *x, int n) {

    int i;
    double sum;

    for(i=0;i<n;i++)
        sum += x[i];

    return sum/n;
}
```

The source code in Listing 7.9 shows the program, analysis, which calls the arithmetic mean function in *mean.c*. Compile *analysis.c* into relocatable object code:

```
$ gcc -c -o analysis.o analysis.c
```

Listing 7.9 *Content of file analysis.c*

```
#include <stdio.h>
#include <stdlib.h>

#define N 100

extern double mean(double *, int);

int main (int argc, char **argv)

{
```

```
int i,n;
double m = 0.0;
double x[N];

if(argc<2) {
    printf ("usage: %s <list values>\n", argv[0]);
    exit(-1);
}

n = argc - 1;

for(i=0;i<n;i++)
    x[i] = atof(argv[i+1]);

m = mean(x,n);
printf("mean: %f\n", m);

return 0;
}
```

We link *analysis.o* and *mean.o* to create the *analysis* binary executable file. As *analysis.o* and *mean.o* are object files, GCC only performs the final linking stage to complete the compilation:

```
$ gcc -Wall -o analysis analysis.o mean.o
```

Verify the resultant executable:

```
$ ./analysis 1 2 3 4 5 6
mean: 3.500000
```

In the example above we linked two object files, namely, *analysis.o* and *mean.o*, to form the binary executable file, *analysis*. If we had many such object files (and typically we could) then linking them all could get somewhat unwieldy. Object files can be compiled into a single archive called a *library*. Libraries come in two forms, namely, static and shared.

Static libraries are created using the archiver utility, ar (which is part of the toolchain). Static library files have the prefix "lib" and the suffix ".a". As with regular object files, static libraries are linked to the program code at compile time.

Shared libraries are libraries that are loaded and linked dynamically by programs when they start (rather than at compile time). When a binary executable runs, the program loader runs. The loader locates and loads all the shared libraries referenced by the executable. The loader locates shared libraries by searching a number of

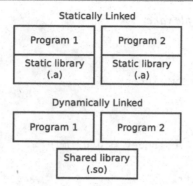

Fig. 7.1 Static versus dynamic libraries

directories. These directories are specified in */etc/ld.so.conf*. Recall we had to create the file */etc/ld.so.conf* in Sect. 6.5.1 of Chap. 6. Shared library directories can also be specified in the LD_LIBRARY_PATH environment variable. Shared library files have a "lib" prefix and a ".so" suffix.

The advantage of shared libraries is that they save memory space. Code from static libraries are stored in the files of the final executable whereas as the code from shared libraries are not. Furthermore, with shared libraries, only one copy of the library code has to be resident in primary memory regardless of how many running programs use it. For each running program that uses static library, there is an instance of it in primary memory. The diagram in Fig. 7.1 illustrates the difference between static and shared libraries.

We present examples of both static and shared libraries. Using the ar command. We create a static library of *statistics* functions. Create a static library using the *mean.o* object file:

```
$ ar r libstat.a mean.o
ar: creating libstat.a
```

Note, the file for the stat[1] library needs to be prefixed with "lib" and suffixed with ".a". The command below shows the modules in the stat library, confirming it contains *mean.o* (only):

```
$ ar t libstat.a
mean.o
```

Now we show how to add a variance function to the stat library. First we create a source code file *var.c* as shown in Listing 7.10.

---

[1]Note that here we use "stat" to denote *statistics* rather than *static* albeit stat is a static library.

Listing 7.10 *Content of file var.c*

```
#include <math.h>

double var(double *x, int n)
{

    int i;
    double sum = 0.0, sqdev = 0.0, mu;

    for(i=0;i<n;i++)
        sum += x[i];

    mu = sum/n;

    for(i=0;i<n;i++)
        sqdev += pow(x[i] - mu, 2.0);

    return sqdev/(n-1);
}
```

Compile the source into object code:

```
$ gcc -Wall -c -o var.o var.c
```

Add the *var.o* module to the stat library:

```
$ ar r libstat.a var.o
$ ar t libstat.a  # display modules in stat libray
mean.o
var.o
```

Now we can extend the functionality of the analysis program to calculate variance as well as the mean. The file *analysis.c* is modified to use the variance function defined in *var.c*. The modified code is shown in Listing 7.11.

Listing 7.11 *Modified content of file analysis.c*

```
#include <stdio.h>
#include <stdlib.h>

#define N 100

extern double mean(double *, int);
```

```
extern double var(double *, int);

int main (int argc, char **argv)

{
    int i,n;
    double m = 0.0, v = 0.0;
    double x[N];

    if(argc<2) {
        printf ("usage: %s <list values>\n", argv[0]);
        exit(-1);
    }

    n = argc - 1;

    for(i=0;i<n;i++)
        x[i] = atof(argv[i+1]);

    m = mean(x,n);
    v = var(x,n);
    printf("mean: %f var: %f\n", m,v);

    return 0;
}
```

Re-compile *analysis.c* with the stat library:

```
$ gcc -Wall -L. -o analysis analysis.c -lstat
```

The stat library is linked to the analysis program using the -l option. We also need to tell GCC the location of library with the -L option. Verify the results of the analysis program:

```
$ ./analysis 1 2 3 4 5 6
mean: 3.500000 var: 3.500000
```

In this example, we compile the analysis program using a shared library. Build the shared library with the command-line below:

```
$ gcc -shared -o libstats.so mean.o var.o
```

We call this library "stats" in order to distinguish it from the static library "stat" that we built earlier. Compile analysis using the stats shared library:

```
$ gcc -o analysis -L. analysis.c -lstats
```

If we run the ldd command on the *analysis* executable file we can see that the stats shared library is referenced:

```
$ ldd analysis
libstats.so => ./libstats.so (0xb785f000)
libc.so.6 => /lib/tls/i686/cmov/libc.so.6 (0xb76e7000)
/lib/ld-linux.so.2 (0xb7864000)
```

If we run the analysis program, it throws an error:

```
$ ./analysis 1 2 3 4 5 6
./analysis: error while loading shared libraries:
libstats.so: cannot open shared object file: No such
file or directory
```

We need to inform the loader of the location of the stats shared library. We could do this by editing the system's */etc/ld.so.conf* file (or any include files referenced within it). For convenience, we use the LD_LIBRARY_PATH environment variable. Add the current directory to LD_LIBRARY_PATH and export it:

```
$ export LD_LIBRARY_PATH=.:$LD_LIBRARY_PATH
```

Now the loader can locate the stats shared library:

```
$ ./analysis 1 2 3 4 5 6
mean: 3.500000 var: 3.500000
```

7.2 Build an ARM Cross Toolchain

Embedded systems are typically low in processing speed and memory (primary and secondary). It is, therefore, unlikely that compilation software will be included as part of an embedded system's own operating system. Embedded system development is performed (typically) on more powerful systems designed for that purpose. The binary images of the toolchain itself must be built for the processor architecture of the host. The toolchain builds binary images for a *target* platform. In the examples shown above, the host and target platforms are the same architecture (Intel x86 architecture). Where host and target are different, a *cross* toolchain is required.

In this section we build a cross compiler for an ARM architecture. While the target machine is ARM, the build machine is x86. The yotta tool is used to cross-compile software written in C++ for the BBC Microbit. The BBC Microbit is an embedded system developed by the BBC for educational use in UK schools. The board has an ARM Cortex-M0 processor and a number of peripherals:

- Accelerometer
- Magnetometer
- Bluetooth
- USB
- 25 LED matrix display

There are also two programmable buttons and five inputs/output connectors that are part of the 23-pin edge connector. The device can be powered by either an external battery pack or micro USB. Programs for the Microbit can be written in a number of languages, Python, Java, Scratch and C++, for example.

We could install yotta natively on our host machine but this presents a problem if we are using an Ubuntu distribution as a host to cross-compile on. The ARM-maintained gcc-arm-embedded package needs to be installed and this necessitates the removal of binutils-arm-none-eabi and gcc-arm-none-eabi packages from the regular repository and a new repository added (that of the ARM maintainers). It is not easy to predict what affect this will have on the development environment of the host. This is what Docker is for, creating development environments that are contained from the host. This section shows how to install yotta in a Docker container.

For this example, we are just going to cross-compile a simple "hello world" program. The source code for the program is shown in Listing 7.12.

Listing 7.12 *Contents of Main.cpp*

```
#include "MicroBit.h"
MicroBit uBit;

int main()
{
    uBit.init();
    uBit.display.scroll("hello world");
    release_fiber();
}
```

Make a directory to work in:

```
$ mkdir microbit && cd microbit
```

Create a Docker file as shown in Listing 7.13

Listing 7.13 *Contents of Dockerfile*

```
FROM ubuntu:16.04

# install required packages
RUN apt-get update && \
        apt-get install -y python-setuptools \
        cmake build-essential \
        ninja-build python-dev \
        libffi-dev libssl-dev \
        srecord \
        software-properties-common

RUN easy_install pip && pip install yotta

RUN apt-get remove -y \
        binutils-arm-none-eabi gcc-arm-none-eabi && \
        add-apt-repository -y \
        ppa:team-gcc-arm-embedded/ppa && \
        apt-get update && \
        apt-get install -y gcc-arm-embedded

ENTRYPOINT ["/bin/bash", "-c", \
            "/usr/local/bin/yotta ${*}", "--"]
```

We build a yotta Docker image with the command-line below:

```
$ docker build -t yotta .
```

Verify the image:

```
$ docker images yotta
REPOSITORY TAG       IMAGE ID       CREATED       SIZE
yotta      latest    edff77eac6d4   2 mins ago    1.1GB
```

Run the yotta init command to create a *module.json* file:

```
$ docker run -v `pwd`:/opt --rm -it yotta init
Enter the module name: <opt> hello
Enter the initial version: <0.0.0> 0.0.1
Is this an executable (instead of a re-usable library
```

```
module)? <no> yes
Short description: Microbit: run yotta in docker
Author: A Holt
What is the license for this project (Apache-2.0,
ISC, MIT etc.)?  <Apache-2.0> MIT
```

The content of the *module.json* files is shown in Listing 7.14.

Listing 7.14 *Contents of module.json*

```
{
    "name": "hello",
    "version": "0.0.1",
    "bin": "./source",
    "private": true,
    "description": "Microbit run yotta in docker",
    "author": "A Holt",
    "license": "MIT",
    "dependencies": {}
}
```

Locate the line below in Listing 7.14:

```
    "dependencies": {}
```

Change the line above so that it looks like this:

```
    "dependencies": {
        "microbit": "lancaster-university/microbit"
    }
```

We need to set the appropriate target so that yotta compiles the source for the BBC
Microbit:

```
$ docker run -v 'pwd':/opt --rm -it \
> yotta target bbc-microbit-classic-gcc
info: get versions for bbc-microbit-classic-gcc
info: download bbc-microbit-classic-gcc@0.2.3 from the
public module registry
info: get versions for mbed-gcc
info: download mbed-gcc@0.1.3 from the public module
registry
```

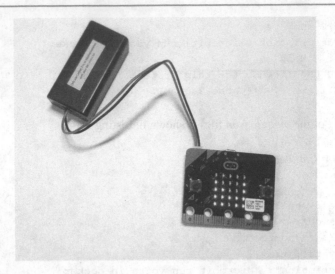

Fig. 7.2 BBC Microbit (powered by battery)

Verify the target:

```
$ docker run -v 'pwd':/opt --rm -it yotta target
bbc-microbit-classic-gcc 0.2.3
mbed-gcc 0.1.3
```

Compile the source code:

```
$ docker run -v 'pwd':/opt --rm -it yotta build
```

This results in a file of object code in *hello-combined.hex*. Connect the Microbit to
the host computer using a USB cable. The Microbit should mount as a filesystem on
the host. In our case, it is mounted on */media/aholt/MICROBIT*. Copy the file to the
Microbit filesystem:

```
$ cd build/bbc-microbit-classic-gcc/source
$ cp hello-combined.hex /media/aholt/MICROBIT
```

Press (and release) the reset button on the Microbit. The text "hello world" will
scroll across the LED display. Figure 7.2 shows the BBC Microbit running our "hello
world" program.

7.3 Summary

In this chapter we have introduced the topic of compiler toolchains. We have, however, avoided an academic treatment of the subject, preferring to present a number of worked examples instead. As the topic of this book is embedded operating systems, we are interested in cross compiler toolchains where the host upon which embedded applications are built are not necessarily the same architecture as the target system.

Summary

In this chapter we have introduced the concept of ...

Embedded ARM Devices

ARM is a family of RISC (reduced instruction set computing) processors that are used extensively in the mobile device market. ARM Holdings plc designs the ARM family of processors but the processors themselves are manufactured by other companies under license. The ARM processor was originally developed by Acorn Computers in collaboration with Apple. Although the acronym, "ARM" stands for advanced RISC machine, it originally stood for *Acorn* RISC machine. Acorn was the company that developed the BBC Micro which was commissioned for The Computer Programme as part of the BBC's "Computer Literacy Project". The BBC Micro was highly successful and was used widely in UK schools. In this chapter we look at two embedded devices based upon the ARM processor, namely, the Raspberry Pi and the BeagleBone.

The Raspberry Pi was designed to be an inexpensive personal computer (sub £30). Despite its small size, the Raspberry Pi features:

- Powerful graphics processor
- USB ports (for mouse and keyboard)
- HDMI port (for a monitor)
- GPIO ports
- Ethernet port (selected models)
- WiFi (selected models)

Like the BBC Micro, the Raspberry Pi was conceived for educational purposes. It is no coincidence that there are A and B versions of the Raspberry Pi just as there were for the BBC Micro. There are a number of GNU/Linux distributions for the Raspberry Pi. The main one is Raspbian which is based upon Debian. Raspbian is a distribution aimed at the desktop market as it includes a graphical user interface. Operating systems, such as Arch Linux or Openwrt (see next section) are more suited to embedded systems.

© Springer International Publishing AG, part of Springer Nature 2018
A. Holt and C.-Y. Huang, *Embedded Operating Systems*, Undergraduate
Topics in Computer Science, https://doi.org/10.1007/978-3-319-72977-0_8

BeagleBones are part of the BeagleBoard series of low-power, open-source hardware, single-board computers. The BeagleBones are produced by Texas Instruments and Digi-Key [1] and are aimed at the educational and hobbyist market. There are two versions of the BeagleBone called the BeagleBone and the BeagleBone Black. The BeagleBone is shipped with the Angstorm GNU/Linux distribution, but can also run Android or Ubuntu (at the time of writing this book).

Both Raspberry Pi and Beaglebones incorporate expansion headers on the board in order to access the general purpose input/output (GPIO) pins. GPIO pins are used in embedded systems to transmit and receive digital signals between peripheral devices.

The Raspberry Pi board has a single 26 pin (2×13 arrangement) expansion header. The BeagleBones has two, 46 pin (in a 2×23 arrangement) expansion headers which are labelled P8 and P9 on the board. As well as general input/output, the GPIO pins can be programmed to provide the following interfaces:

- Inter-integrated Circuit (I^2C)
- Serial peripheral interface (SPI)
- Universal asynchronous receiver/transmitter (UART)

Pins for +3.3 V, +5 V and GND supply lines are also available from expansion headers.

This chapter is organised into two sections, one for each system. We show how to get started with each system and how to access them. We also take the opportunity to explore the physical computing features they provide.

8.1   Raspberry Pi

The Raspberry Pi is a small form factor desktop PC but is also suited to embedded applications. The board features a Broadcom (system on a chip) processor. It also includes a Videocore 4 GPU which is capable of BluRay quality playback. There were, initially, two models of Raspberry Pi, namely, the model A and model B (a reference back to BBC Micro models). Since the first A and B models were introduced, there have been a number of new models and revisions. Table 8.1 compares their specifications. Figure 8.1 shows a photograph of the original A and B models.

8.1.1   Installing an Operating System

At the time of writing this book, the Raspberry Pi supports a number of operating systems:

- Raspbian: Debian for Raspberry Pi.
- Arch Linux: Arch Linux is a simple, lightweight GNU/Linux distribution.

Table 8.1 Raspberry Pi models

Model	Architecture	Speed	Memory	Ethernet	WiFi
Zero	ARMv6Z (32-bit)	1 GHz	512 MB	No	No
Zero/w	ARMv6Z (32-bit)	1 GHz	512 MB	No	Yes
A	ARMv6Z (32-bit)	700 MHz	256 MB	No	No
B (and B+)	ARMv6Z (32-bit)	700 MHz	512 MB	No	No
2B	ARMv7-A (32-bit)	900 MHz	1 GB	10/100	No
2B (v1.2)	ARMv8-A (64/32-bit)	900 MHz	1 GB	10/100	No
3B	ARMv8-A (64/32-bit)	1.2 GHz	1 GB	10/100	Yes

Fig. 8.1 Raspberry Pi. Model A (left), Model B (right)

- Android: Google's smart phone and tablet OS.
- Risc OS: RISC OS [2,3] was designed by Acorn Computers Ltd to run on the ARM chipset.
- Plan 9: Plan 9 from the Bell Labs [4] is an operating system developed by the Bell Laboratories as a successor to Unix. It is primarily for researchers and hobbyists.
- Openwrt: Openwrt (and a fork of Openwrt, LEDE) is a framework for building embedded firmware images for many platform architectures.

Download the latest version of Raspbian (which, at the time of writing this book is Jessie):

```
$ wget http://downloads.raspberrypi.org/raspbian_latest
```

Uncompress the image file:

```
$ mv raspbian_latest jessie.zip
$ unzip jessie.zip
Archive:  jessie.zip
inflating: 2017-07-05-raspbian-jessie.img
```

Connect the SD card to the host machine (you may need an SD card reader) and unmount any filesystems that automatically mounted. Write the image to the SD card:

```
$ sudo dd if=2017-07-05-raspbian-jessie.img \
> of=/dev/sdb bs=1M
850+0 records in
1850+0 records out
1939865600 bytes (1.9 GB) copied, 509.074 s, 3.8 MB/s
```

Remove the SD card from the host PC and insert into the SD slot of the Raspberry Pi. When the Raspberry Pi is powered on the operating system will boot.

8.1.2   Using the Raspberry Pi Serial Port

In this subsection, we present a simple exercise with the Raspberry Pi's GPIO ports. We show how to connect to the Raspberry Pi through its serial port. This is useful if the unit is a model A. The model A lacks an Ethernet port which prevents remote access to the command-line[1] and would otherwise need a monitor, keyboard and mouse. The aim of this exercise is to show how the Raspberry Pi's serial port can be accessed using a USB serial port of a PC.

The serial port is accessible through the GPIO ports 14 and 15, which are the serial transmit (TXD) and receive (RXD) respectively. There are a number of ways of connecting a serial USB to the Raspberry Pi's GPIO ports. Probably the easiest way is to use a console lead. The console lead in [5] has female connectors which can be plugged onto the GPIO pins directly but we use a Arduino Uno as an *interface* between the USB interface and the GPIO pins. A list of components used are given below:

- Raspberry Pi. In this exercise we used a Model A, but any of the models could be used. The voltages on GPIO pins should not exceed 3.3V, otherwise the Raspberry Pi could be damaged. For this reason, care should be taken when connecting to the GPIOs.

---

[1] We use an 802.11n USB adapter and access the device over WiFi.

- Slice of Pi: Break out board for the Raspberry Pi [6]. We use the break out board as a convenient way to connect to the GPIO pins. Note that, the pin headers need to be soldered to the PCB.
- Arduino. We used an Arduino Uno as it has pin headers for the GPIOs.
- 2 × USB cables:

  - Type-A to type-B cable USB for communication between the PC and Arduino. This also provides power to the Arduino.
  - Type-A to type-B Micro to provide power to the Raspberry Pi.

- An assortment of jumper cables.

We need to download a blank sketch to the Arduino so that the bootloader does not respond to activity on the USB serial interface. Listing 8.1 shows the code for the sketch.

Listing 8.1 *Blank sketch for the Arduino*

```
void setup() {
}
void loop() {
}
```

In order to compile and download the sketch to the arduino, it is necessary to install the Arduino IDE (integrated development environment) on the host. Download the latest Adrduino IDE (at the time of writing this book, the latest release is 1.5.4):

```
$ cd arduino-1.5.4
$ ./arduino
```

Connect the Arduino to the host PC using the appropriate USB cable. Run the dmesg command on the host, you should see a line like this:

```
[ 6094.178626] cdc_acm 5-1:1.0: ttyACM0: USB ACM device
```

This tells us the Arduino is connected to the */dev/ttyACM0* device. Run the Arduino IDE and enter the code in Listing 8.1. Figure 8.2 shows the IDE with sketch code entered. Ensure that the IDE is connected to the correct serial devices. (*/dev/ttyACM0* in our case). Click on the Tools tab and from the drop down menu, select the Serial Port menu item. Select the serial device on which the Arduino is connected. Next, we set the Arduino board type. From the Tools drop down menu, select the Board menu option. From here, configure the IDE for the appropriate Arduino (in our case, this is an Arduino Uno).

Compile the sketch by clicking on the button marked with a "√". If the compilation is successful, download the compiled sketch to the Arduino by clicking on the "→" button. The IDE can now be closed down.

With the Raspberry Pi powered off (USB disconnected) attach the Slice of Pi break out board. Then connect the RX pin on the Arduino (digital pin 0) to TX on the Raspberry Pi. Similarly connect the Arduino TX pin (digital pin 1) to the Raspberry

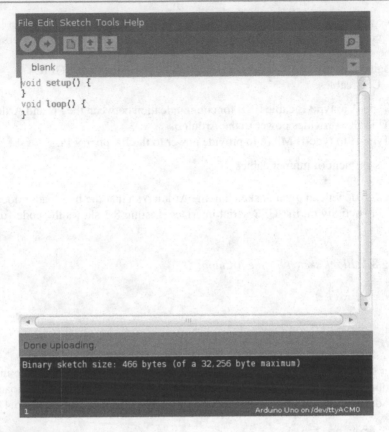

Fig. 8.2 Arduino IDE

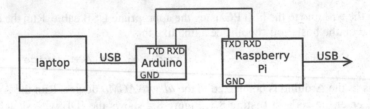

Fig. 8.3 Raspberry Pi serial connection

Pi's RX pin. Finally connect the ground (GND) pins of both units. The diagram in
Fig. 8.3 shows a schematic of the connection between the Arduino and Raspberry Pi
(but at this stage, the USB to the Raspberry Pi should not be connected). On the host
PC, run a terminal emulator:

```
$ sudo minicom -b 115200 -D /dev/ttyACM0
```

Power up the Raspberry Pi by connecting the USB cable. Kernel messages should
start streaming to the screen as the device boots up. After the start up scripts have

run, a login prompt should appear. Login with the user account name "pi" and default password "raspberry":

```
raspberrypi login: pi
Password: raspberry
pi@raspberrypi:~$
```

If this is the first time that the Raspberry pi has been booted, then a message will be displayed stating the configuration is incomplete. Run the configuration utility below:

```
$ sudo raspi-config
```

This displays a menu of options for customising the Raspberry Pi (Fig. 8.4). We recommend you select option 1, so the filesystem size is expanded to the full size of the SD card.

Secure shell (SSH) can be enabled/disabled through the Advanced options (option 8). In our case we are using a model A which does not have an Ethernet port. For this reason we leave SSH disabled. If you have a model B (which has an Ethernet port) or you have a USB WiFi device (which can be used with a model A) then you may wish to enable SSH.

The Raspberry Pi uses NTP (network time protocol) by default to sync its clock. As our device lacks a network connection we found the time was several months out. We, therefore, set the date manually:

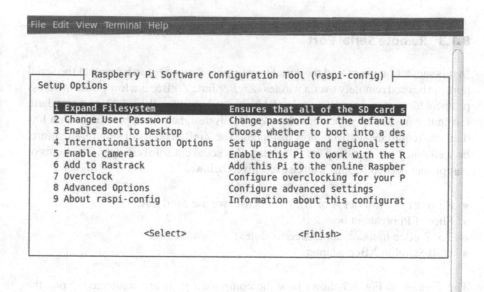

Fig. 8.4 Raspberry Pi initial configuration menu

```
pi@raspberrypi:@$ sudo date -s "27 JUN 2013 14:33:00"
Thu Jun 27 14:33:00 BST 2013
```

We also disabled the NTP daemon (if you have a Raspberry Pi with network capabilities we suggest you omit these steps). Make the directory for runlevel 2 scripts
the current directory:

```
pi@raspberrypi:@$ cd /etc/rc2.d
```

In this directory there should be a symbolic link to the NTP start-up script in
/etc/init.d/:

```
pi@raspberrypi:/etc/rc2.d$ ls *ntp
S02ntp
```

Change the name of the symbolic link so that it begins with a "K":

```
pi@raspberrypi:/etc/rc2.d$ sudo mv S02ntp K02ntp
```

Run the update-rc.d script, but ignore any errors:

```
pi@raspberrypi:/etc/rc2.d$i sudo update-rc.d script
        defaults
update-rc.d: using dependency based boot sequencing
update-rc.d: error: unable to read /etc/init.d/script
```

Reboot the unit:

```
$ sudo shutdown -r now
```

8.1.3   Remote Serial Port

In this subsection we extend the serial port exercise from Sect. 8.1.2 so that the serial
port can be used remotely over a wireless *ZigBee* link. ZigBee is a low power wireless
protocol for personal area networks (PANs) based upon the IEEE 802.15.4 standard.
Given that transmission power is low, ZigBee is designed for applications with low
data rate requirements over short distances. The ZigBee protocol should, therefore,
be well suited for accessing the Raspberry Pi's serial console remotely. The items of
equipiment needed for this exercise are given below.

- Raspberry Pi (Model A or B). In our case, we use Model A.
- Slice of Pi breakout board.
- 2 × ZigBee transceivers (XBee modules).
- USB Serial to XBee adapter.

The diagram in Fig. 8.5 shows how the component parts are connected. Note, the
dotted line represents a wireless link.
    The Slice of Pi breakout board connects to the expansion headers of the Rapsberry
Pi. There are expansion headers on the Slice of Pi for the XBee module. Figure 8.6

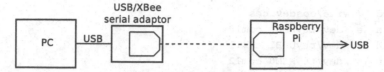

Fig. 8.5 Raspberry Pi remote serial connection over ZigBee

Fig. 8.6 XBee module attached to Raspberry Pi

shows how the XBee module interfaces to the Raspberry Pi using the Slice of Pi breakout board.

Configuration of the XBee modules is performed using a utility called X-CTU (which is free to download). Unfortunately, there is only a Windows version of the X CTU available but it is possible to run X-CTU on a GNU/Linux system under Wine (Wine is not an emulator). Wine can be installed using the package management system. On Debian and derivatives, use:

```
$ sudo apt-get install wine
```

Download the X-CTU installer utility:

```
$ wget http://ftp1.digi.com/support/utilities/\
> 40003002_B.exe
```

As X-CTU is a Microsoft Windows application, it uses Windows nomenclature to specify the devices serial ports, namely, COM1, COM2 etc, whereas GNU/Linux uses file object pathnames to reference devices. In the *dosdrives* directory, create a number of symbolic links that the serial devices we are likely use:

```
$ cd ~/.wine/dosdevices
$ ln -s /dev/ttyUSB0 com10
$ ln -s /dev/ttyUSB1 com11
$ ln -s /dev/ttyACM0 com12
```

We need to configure the two XBee modules for different roles. One module is configured as the *coordinator* and the other as a *router*. Each module has a unique 64 bit serial number which we will use in the configuration procedure. The serial numbers are printed on the underside of the module. The 32 most significant bits (msb) of the serial number for XBee modules is 0013A200. The 32 least significant bits (lsb) are unique to the module.

Choose one module to be configured as the coordinator and one to be configured as the router (the choice is arbitrary). Make a note of the respective serial numbers. Table 8.2 shows the serial numbers for the coordinator and router of our modules (the serial number for your modules will be different). When we configure the modules, we use the serial number of the router as the destination address in the coordinator and vice versa. This will become apparent when we describe the configuration process but you should ensure you have these serial numbers to hand when you perform it.

We will begin with the coordinator. Start the X-CTU utility. A window like the one in Fig. 8.7 is displayed on the screen.

We must first establish communication with the XBee module. Connect the host to the XBee module using the USB serial converter [7] (and USB cable). Figure 8.8 shows the XBee module seated in the expansion headers of the USB to serial converter.

Check dmesg to see which serial port the XBee module attaches to. In our case, it is */dev/ttyUSB0* which we defined as *com10*. Select the User Com Ports tab in X-CTU (Fig. 8.9). In the Com Port Number text box, enter "COM10" (characters are displayed in upper case regardless of the case they are entered) and click the Add button. "COM10" will appear as an option in the Select Com Port box.

Click on COM10 in the Select Com Port box to highlight it. Then select the Test/Query button. If the test is successful, you should see a message window similar to one in Fig. 8.9.

- Check that pins are correctly seated in the sockets. It is easy to insert the XBee module with the pins misaligned in the sockets.
- Check the XBee unit is connected correctly. Did a message appear in dmesg?
- Check the serial port is correct (dmesg).

Table 8.2 XBee Serial Numbers

Role	32-msb	32-lsb
Coordinator	0013A200	408A8966
Router	0013A200	408A8957

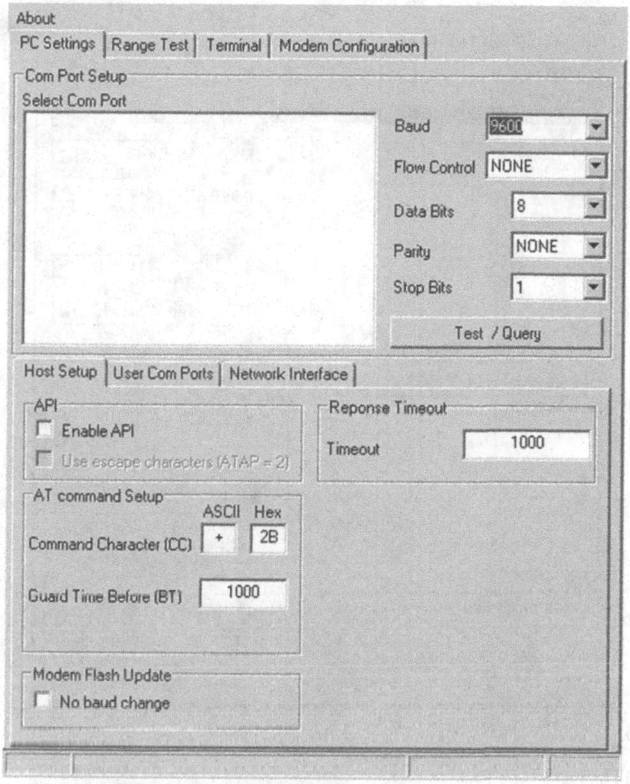

About

PC Settings | Range Test | Terminal | Modem Configuration |

Com Port Setup

Select Com Port

Baud 9600

Flow Control NONE

Data Bits 8

Parity NONE

Stop Bits 1

Test / Query

Host Setup | User Com Ports | Network Interface |

API

☐ Enable API

☐ Use escape characters (ATAP = 2)

Reponse Timeout

Timeout 1000

AT command Setup

ASCII Hex

Command Character (CC) +   2B

Guard Time Before (BT) 1000

Modem Flash Update

☐ No baud change

Fig. 8.7 X-CTU

Fig. 8.8 The XBee module connected to USB serial converter

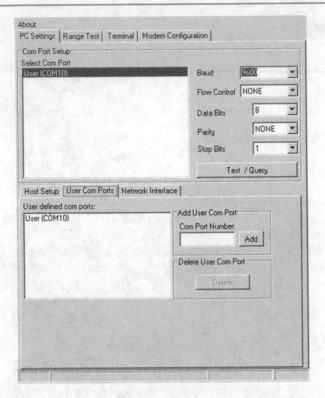

Fig. 8.10 X-CTU Modem Query

- Check the symbolic links in *dosdrives* point to the correct interfaces?
- Check that the communication parameters are correct. The default communication parameters for the XBee modules are 9600 baud, 8-bits, no parity. As we can see from Fig. 8.9, the settings in X-CTU reflect the default settings. If the parameters on the XBee module have been changed then set them accordingly.

As well as confirming communication between the PC and XBee modules (Fig. 8.10), the Test/Query Modem dialogue box also gives us other information about the module, namely:

- Modem type: XB24-B
- Modem firmware version: 1020
- Serial Number: 13A200408A8966

Select the Modem Configuration tab. Click the Read button. X-CTU will read the parameters from the module.

Modem Type: The modem type for our module is XB24-B but we can upgrade it to the XB24-ZB firmware. Click on the down arrow of the Modem XBee and select "XB24-ZB" from the drop down menu.

Function Set: Configure this module as a coordinator. Under Function Set, bring up the drop down menu and select "ZIGBEE COORDINATOR AT".

Baud rate: The baud rate of the module needs to match that of the Raspberry Pi serial port, which is 115200 baud. In the panel with the scroll bar, scroll down to the Serial Interface section. There is a parameter for the baud Rate. From the drop down menu for baud Rate, select 115200.

Destination address: The destination address is a serial number of the *other* router. As we are configuring the coordinator here, these fields must contain the serial number of the router. The destination address is divided into two components, namely, DH and DL. In the DH field enter the most significant 128 bits of the router's serial number: 13A200 (the leading zero can be omitted). In the DL field, enter the least significant bits of the router's serial number. In our case, this is 408A8957 (see Table 8.2).

On completion of the steps above, click the Write button to download the parameters to the module. As we are upgrading the firmware, a dialogue box is displayed similar to the one shown in Fig. 8.11. Respond to this dialogue box by pressing and releasing the reset button on the module. The firmware download will then resume.

Fig. 8.11   X-CTU Info

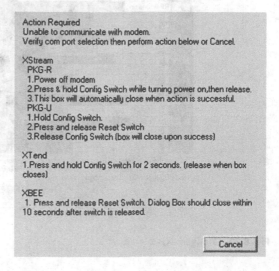

Action Required
Unable to communicate with modem.
Verify com port selection then perform action below or Cancel.

XStream
  PKG-R
  1.Power off modem
  2.Press & hold Config Switch while turning power on,then release.
  3.This box will automatically close when action is successful.
  PKG-U
  1.Hold Config Switch.
  2.Press and release Reset Switch
  3.Release Config Switch (box will close upon success)

XTend
1.Press and hold Config Switch for 2 seconds. (release when box closes)

XBEE
  1. Press and release Reset Switch. Dialog Box should close within 10 seconds after switch is released.

Cancel

On successful completion of the firmware download, we recommend returning to the PC Settings tab to run a Test/Query on the module. Ensure you change the baud rate setting to 115200. This completes the configuration of the coordinator. The procedure for configuring the router/end device module is similar to that of the coordinator. Just as with the coordinator set Modem XBee to "XB24-ZB" and baud rate to 115200. However, for the Function Set, select "ZIGBEE ROUTER DEVICE AT". Set DH and DL (destination address) to 0013A200 and 408A8966 respectively (where, for the DL field you should substitute the 32-lsb for your XBee router module. Click the Write button to download the firmware to module (Fig. 8.12).

Power off the Raspberry Pi, then connect one of the XBee modules to it using the break out box. Either module can be used here, but we used the XBee module configured as the router. Connect the other XBee module (in our case the coordinator) to the PC with the XBee adapter and the USB cable. Run the terminal emulator:

```
$ sudo minicom -b 115200 -D /dev/ttyUSB0
```

A preliminary test of the XBee module can be performed by typing +++. An OK message should be displayed on the screen. This places the module into command

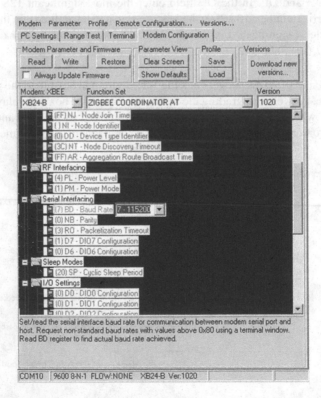

Fig. 8.12 Configure XBee

mode. The modules understand AT-like commands just like a regular modem. We can query the destination address with the ATDH and ATDL commands which display the respective 32-msb and 32-lsb of the destination address:

```
atdh
13A200
atdl
408A8957
```

This confirms the destination address of the coordinator is that of the router. You should note, that after a few seconds of inactivity, the mode will revert back to transparent. If you wish to enter mode AT commands, you will need to type +++ again.

Power up the Raspberry Pi. After a few seconds the kernel messages will be displayed on the screen. Once the boot process has completed the login prompt will appear.

```
Debian GNU/Linux 7.0 raspberrypi ttyAMA0

raspberrypi login:
```

8.2 BeagleBone

In this section we show how to set up both the BeagleBone and BeagleBone Black (see Fig. 8.13). We also give a brief introduction into physical computing programming on BeagleBones. BeagelBones are *bare bones* versions of the BeagleBoard series. Their technical specification is shown in Table 8.3 (the table also shows the specification of the other BeagleBoards, though we do not cover them in this book).

8.2.1 Setting up the BeagleBone

In this subsection we describe how to get the BeagleBone devices working. In order to avoid confusion, we use the terms *original BeagleBone* and *BeagleBone Black* to distinguish between the respective models. The term *BeagleBone* refers to either model when the distinction is unimportant. There are small differences between the set up of the original BeagleBone and the BeagleBone Black which we will cover in this section.

Connect the BeagleBone to a personal computer (running GNU/Linux) using a USB cable. Run the dmesg command. If you are using an original BeagleBone, then you will see a line similar to the one below:

```
[10791.561172] usb 2-1.1: FTDI USB Serial Device
converter now attached to ttyUSB0
```

Fig. 8.13 Original BeagleBone (left) and BeagleBone Black (right)

Table 8.3 BeagleBoards technical specification

Board	Processor	Speed	Memory
BeagleBoard	OMAP3530 ARM Cortex-A8	720 MHz	256 MB
BeagleBoard-xM	AM37x ARM Cortex-A8 compatible	1 GHz	512 MB
BeagleBone	AM335x ARM Cortex-A8	720 MHz	256 MB
BeagleBone Black	AM335x ARM Cortex-A8	1 GHz	512 MB

This tells us that the BeagleBone is connected to the */dev/ttyUSB0* serial device.
For BeagleBone Black, the host uses a different device driver. The line in the dmesg
results shows that the host is connected to the BeagleBone Black using */dev/ttyACM0*:

```
[ 7944.956365] cdc_acm 2-1:1.2: ttyACM0: USB ACM device
```

Use the command below to connect to the BeagleBone's serial console, ensuring that
you use the appropriate console device:

```
$ sudo minicom -b 115200 -D /dev/ttyUSB0
```

A banner and the login prompt is displayed. In this example, we are using an original
BeagleBone running the Angstrom distribution it came with:

```
.---0---.
|       |                          .-.                 o o
|   |   |-----.-----.-----.| |   .----..-----.-----.
|       |     | --- | ---'| |'--.|  .-'|     |     |
|   |   |  |  | --- ||  --'|  |  |  |  |  ' | | | | |
'---'---'--'--'--.  |-----''----''--'  '-----'-'-'-'
             _'  |
              '---'
```

```
The Angstrom Distribution beaglebone tty00

Angstrom v2012.01-core - Kernel 3.2.5+

beaglebone login: root
Last login: Thu Mar 15 15:21:52 UTC 2012 on tty00
root@beaglebone:~#
```

At this point, we recommend you give the root account a password (using the passwd
command). As well as providing a serial connection over the USB interface the
BeagleBone comes up as a mass storage device on the host PC:

```
$ mount      # Run no host
/dev/sdb on /media/BEAGLE_BONE type vfat (rw,nosuid,
nodev,uhelper=udisks,uid=1000,gid=1000,shortname=
mixed,dmask=0077,utf8=1,flush)
```

This USB interface can also be used for IP networking. The difference between the
two models is that the BeagleBone Black can support both services simultaneously
whereas the original BeagleBone can only support one or the other. If we look at
the modules on the original BeagleBone, we see the g_mass_storage module is
currently loaded:

```
root@beaglebone:~# lsmod
Module                 Size  Used by
g_mass_storage        24010  0
ipv6                 210434  16
```

In order to establish networking between the host PC and the original BeagleBone
we need to eject the storage device on the host:

```
$ sudo eject /dev/sdb
```

It is important to note that it is not necessary to eject the storage device with
the BeagleBone Black, the network interfaces will be brought up automatically
when the device boots. Returning to the original BeagleBone, we see that the
g_mass_storage has been replaced by the g_ether module:

```
root@beaglebone:~# lsmod
Module                  Size  Used by
g_ether                 27775  0
ipv6                    210434 16
```

This has the effect of bringing up a usb0 Ethernet interface on the original Beagle-Bone (on the BeagleBone Black the usb0 will come up automatically):

```
root@beaglebone:~# ifconfig usb0
usb0      Link encap:Ethernet   HWaddr BE:4C:75:39:6E:08
          inet addr:192.168.7.2  Bcast:192.168.7.3
Mask:255.255.255.252
          inet6 addr: fe80::bc4c:75ff:fe39:6e08/64
Scope:Link
          UP BROADCAST RUNNING MULTICAST  MTU:1500
Metric:1
          RX packets:19 errors:0 dropped:0 overruns:0
frame:0
          TX packets:30 errors:0 dropped:0 overruns:0
carrier:0
          collisions:0 txqueuelen:1000
          RX bytes:5214 (5.0 KiB)  TX bytes:5748
(5.6 KiB)
```

A corresponding Ethernet interface is brought up on the host PC:

```
$ ifconfig eth2
eth2      Link encap:Ethernet   HWaddr d4:94:a1:8b:39:99
          inet addr:192.168.7.1  Bcast:192.168.7.3
Mask:255.255.255.252
          inet6 addr: fe80::d694:a1ff:fe8b:3999/64
Scope:Link
          UP BROADCAST RUNNING MULTICAST  MTU:1500
Metric:1
          RX packets:30 errors:0 dropped:0 overruns:0
frame:0
          TX packets:19 errors:0 dropped:0 overruns:0
carrier:0
          collisions:0 txqueuelen:1000
          RX bytes:5328 (5.3 KB)  TX bytes:5480 (5.4 KB)
```

From the BeagleBone (original or Black edition), we can verify that there is a network connection between the target and the host with the Ping command:

```
root@beaglebone:~# ping -c 4 -q 192.168.7.1
PING 192.168.7.1 (192.168.7.1) 56(84) bytes of data.
```

```
--- 192.168.7.1 ping statistics ---
4 packets transmitted, 4 received, 0% packet loss,
time 2998ms
rtt min/avg/max/mdev = 0.233/0.290/0.338/0.041 ms
```

Attempts to connect to systems beyond the host, will fail:

```
root@beaglebone:~# ping -c 4 -q 8.8.8.8
PING 8.8.8.8 (8.8.8.8) 56(84) bytes of data.

--- 8.8.8.8 ping statistics ---
4 packets transmitted, 0 received, 100% packet loss,
time 3001ms
```

This is because the network infrastructure the host is connected to does not have a
route to network 192.168.7.0/24. We can resolve the issue by implementing NAT
(network address translation) on the host. Enable IP packet forwarding so that the
host can forward packets between usb0 and its Ethernet port (in our case eth0):

```
$ sudo -i
# echo 1 > /proc/sys/net/ipv4/ip_forward
# exit
logout
```

On the host, configure NAT using the following sequences of iptables commands:

```
$ iptables -F
$ iptables -A INPUT -i lo -j ACCEPT
$ iptables -A POSTROUTING -t nat -o eth0 \
> -s 192.168.7.0/24 -d 0/0  -j MASQUERADE
$ iptables -A FORWARD -t filter -o eth0 -m state \
> --state NEW,ESTABLISHED,RELATED -j ACCEPT
$ iptables -A FORWARD -t filter -i eth2 -m state \
> --state ESTABLISHED,RELATED -j ACCEPT
```

The BeagleBone can now communicate with the external network. We should emphasise that, networking using the USB interface is just one option. Both the BeagelBones
have regular Ethernet interfaces which can be configured for IP.

8.2.2 Physical Computer Programming on the BeagleBone

The BeagleBones have a number of GPIO (general purpose input/output) pins and
LEDs, which are programmable. To illustrate physical computer programming on
the BeagleBone we present a simple example on how to interact with the four USER
LEDs. The USER LEDs are located near the S3 power switch and are labelled USER
1 through to 4 on the board. The LEDs (and GPIOs) can be controlled by writing to

files in sysfs. For brevity, define the pathname to the directory for the BeagleBone's
LEDs:

```
root@beaglebone:~# LEDSPATH=\
> "/sys/devices/platform/leds-gpio/leds/
```

If we examine the contents of the $LEDSPATH directory, we see a subdirectory for
each of the LEDs:

```
root@beaglebone:~# ls ${LEDSPATH}
beaglebone::usr0  beaglebone::usr1  beaglebone::usr2
beaglebone::usr3
```

Directories are labelled 0 to 3 and correspond to USER LEDs 1 to 4 respectively.
These directories contain files, subdirectories and symbolic links which relate to the
individual LEDs. Choosing, USER LED 4, for example:

```
root@beaglebone:~# ls ${LEDPATH}/beaglebone::usr3
brightness  device  max_brightness  power  subsystem
trigger  uevent
```

We can turn LEDs on and off by changing the content of the *brightness* file. For
example, USER LED 4 can be turned on by writing a "1" to the corresponding
brightness file:

```
echo $1 > ${GPIOPATH}/beaglebone\:\:usr3/brightness
```

Conversely, writing a "0" to the corresponding *brightness* file turns LED 4 off:

```
echo $1 > ${GPIOPATH}/beaglebone\:\:usr3/brightness
```

The Python code in Listing 8.2 shows a script for turning the LEDs on then off in
a repeated sequence. It defines a UserLED class that, when declared, initialises the
LEDs (turns them off). The UserLED class supports methods for turning the LEDs
both on and off by writing to LED the *brightness* files in sysfs.

Listing 8.2 *Contents of led_seq.py*

```
#!/usr/bin/env python

import sys,time

ledpath = "/sys/devices/platform/leds-gpio/leds"

class UserLED():

    def __init__(self, n):
```

```
            self.led = "%s/beaglebone::usr%d/brightness" % \
                       (ledpath,n)
            self.clear()

    def set(self):
        open(self.led, 'w').write("1")

    def clear(self):
        open(self.led, 'w').write("0")


def led_seq():
    for method in ["set", "clear"]:
        for i in xrange(4):
            led = "USR%d.%s()" % (i,method)

if __name__=='__main__':

    # Declare LED objects
    USR0 = UserLED(0)
    USR1 = UserLED(1)
    USR2 = UserLED(2)
    USR3 = UserLED(3)

    while True:
        led_seq()
```

Create a file *led_seq.py* with the contents of Listing 8.2 and give it execute permissions:

```
root@beaglebone:~# chmod +x led_seq.py
```

Run the script:

```
root@beaglebone:~# ./led_seq.py
```

The USER LEDs will blink on and off in a repeated sequence. Now we show how to program the BeagleBone using the system's IDE (integrated development environment). The BeagleBone and BeagleBone Black both come with an IDE called Cloud9. We demonstrate how to use the Cloud9 IDE to program the physical hardware of the BeagleBone.

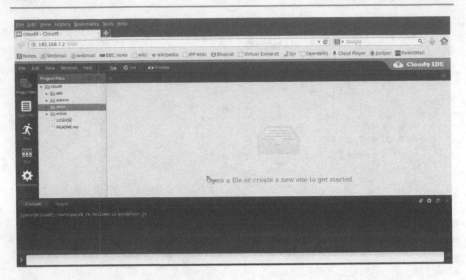

Fig. 8.14   Cloud9, IDE for the BeagleBone

The programming language supported by Cloud9 is JavaScript. It comes with the Bonescript library which provides an API to control the physical hardware (GPIOs and LEDs). Bonescript is an optimised Node.js library for BeagleBoards. Node.js was designed for developing scalable network applications by using non-blocking, event-driven I/O. I/O requests to the BeagleBone's physical hardware are implemented as asynchronous *callbacks*. An event loop runs and executes the corresponding callback function for each event as it occurs. The advantage of this programming method, is that the program does not block on I/O requests.

Cloud9 can be accessed using a Web browser by entering the URL: 192.168.7.2: 3000. When using Cloud9 for the first time, a dialogue box is displayed from which you can select a detailed guided tour of the IDE. It is a good idea to take the guided tour at some point, but for now, just click the button "Just the editor, please". Figure 8.14 shows the Cloud9 IDE running in a Web browser.

The program in Listing 8.3 shows the JavaScript code to interact with the four USER LEDs on the board. This will control the LEDs in the same way as the Python script in Listing 8.2. Create a new project by clicking on the + in the projects tab. Enter the code in Listing 8.3 into the new tab (see Fig. 8.15). Then save the project to a file by pressing CONTROL-S. You will be prompted to give the file a name. In this example, we call it *led_seq.js* and save it in the *demo* directory. Execute the program by clicking on the "run" icon in the top menu bar. The "run" icon is replaced by a "stop" icon (which can be used to terminate the program).

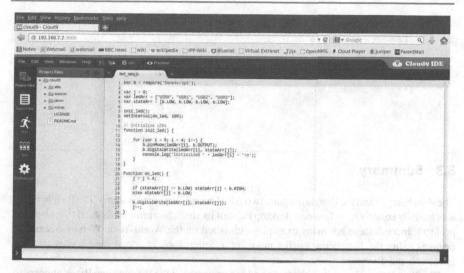

Fig. 8.15 Cloud9

Listing 8.3 *BeagleBone Black LED example*

```
var b = require('bonescript');

var j = 0;
var ledArr = ["USR0", "USR1", "USR2", "USR3"];
var stateArr = [b.LOW, b.LOW, b.LOW, b.LOW];

init_led();
setInterval(do_led, 100);

// Initialise LEDs
function init_led() {

    for (var i = 0; i < 4; i++) {
        b.pinMode(ledArr[i], b.OUTPUT);
        b.digitalWrite(ledArr[i], stateArr[j]);
        console.log('Initialised ' + ledArr[i] + '\n');
    }

}

// Toggle LEDs
function do_led() {
    j = j % 4;
```

```
    if (stateArr[j] == b.LOW) stateArr[j] = b.HIGH;
    else stateArr[j] = b.LOW;

    b.digitalWrite(ledArr[j], stateArr[j]);
    j++;
}
```

8.3 Summary

The Raspberry Pi and the BeagleBone are two ARM based computer systems. The Raspberry Pi was initially conceived as low-cost desktop PC, but its small footprint lends itself to embedded projects. Indeed, there are many examples published on the World-Wide Web of embedded projects using the Raspberry Pi (for more information look at social media sites such as Facebook and Twitter).

The BeagleBone is more suited to embedded projects but the BeagleBone Black appears to be aimed specifically at the Raspberry Pi market, as it can also operate as a personal computer.

References

1. BeagleBoard (2013) BeagleBoard.org—community support open hardware. Accessed 14 May 2013
2. RISC OS Open (2013) RISC OS Open. https://www.riscosopen.org/content. Accessed 21 June 2013
3. RISC OS Org (2013) RISC OS Org. http://www.riscos.org.uk. Accessed 21 June 2013
4. Pike R, Presotto D, Thompson K, Trickey H (1990) Plan 9 from bell labs. In: Proceedings of the summer 1990 UKUUG conference. pp 1–9
5. Adafruit (2013) Adafruit's Raspberry Pi Lesson 5. Using a console cable. http://learn.adafruit.com/adafruits-raspberry-pi-lesson-5-using-a-console-cable/connect-the-lead. Accessed 25 June 2013
6. MODMYPI (2013) Slice of Pi—Raspberry Pi breakout board. https://www.modmypi.com/slice-of-pi-raspberry-pi-breakout-boad. Accessed 25 June 2013
7. Cool Components (2013) UartSBee V4—XBee Adapter. http://www.coolcomponents.co.uk/catalog/uartsbee-xbee-adapter-p-980.html. Accessed 2 July 2013

Openwrt

9

Openwrt is a GNU/Linux distribution for embedded systems. However, it is not merely a static firmware image, it is a complete framework for building customised firmware images. The images comprise a bootloader, kernel, root filesystem and applications.

The Openwrt project began as a means of developing third party firmware for The Linksys WRT54G devices. The Linksys WRT54G is a home router with a built-in firewall and WiFi access-point. There are a number of variants, namely the WRT54GL and WRTSL54GS. The significance of this product is that it used General Public License (GPL) code for its firmware. Given this, Linksys were "encouraged" to release this firmware back into the community, pursuant with the license. This enabled the community to build their own firmware images for WRT54G devices. Openwrt, as well as several other projects, was developed for the purpose of building WRT54G firmware images. Openwrt, however, is not limited to just Linksys WRT54G routers, it supports a plethora of embedded devices, see [1] for a comprehensive list. At the time of writing this book, there are a number of branches Openwrt which are listed in Table 9.1.

In this chapter we introduce two devices which can run Openwrt:

- Open-mesh
- Dragino

Both units are based upon the MIPS processor (microprocessor without interlocked pipeline stages). The MIPS processor is a RISC architecture developed by MIPS Technologies. MIPS processors are used widely in embedded environments and are often used in educational environments for the purpose of studying microprocessors.

Open-mesh is sold as a commercial mesh WiFi solution but it is possible to reflash devices with firmware for a customised embedded application. The Dragino is a similar device to the Open-mesh but more aimed at the Arduino Yùn market

© Springer International Publishing AG, part of Springer Nature 2018 195
A. Holt and C.-Y. Huang, *Embedded Operating Systems*, Undergraduate
Topics in Computer Science, https://doi.org/10.1007/978-3-319-72977-0_9

Table 9.1 Branches of Openwrt (at the time of writing this book)

Name	Version	Kernel
White Russian	0.9	2.4
Kamikaze	7.06–8.09.2	2.6
Backfire	10.03 and 10.03.1	2.6.32
Attitude adjustment	12.09	3.3
Barrier breaker	14.07	3.14
Chaos calmer	15.05	3.18.23

which is a device that combines a microcontroller with a WiFi system on a chip (SoC) that can run GNU/Linux.

9.1 Openwrt UML

Before building Openwrt firmware for an actual hardware platform, we will build an Openwrt UML kernel and root filesystem. Create a directory to work in:

```
$ mkdir ~/openwrt_uml && cd ~/openwrt_uml
```

The Openwrt Buildroot comprises a set of Makefiles and patches for building a cross-compiler toolchain and a root filesystem for the target system. Download the Openwrt Buildroot by cloning the git repository:

```
$ git clone git://github.com/openwrt/openwrt.git
Cloning into 'openwrt'...
```

Change to the *openwrt* directory that has been created:

```
$ cd openwrt/
```

The Openwrt Buildroot consists of a number of feeds where each feed is a collection of packages. Install Openwrt feeds by running the feeds update script:

```
$ ./scripts/feeds update -a
```

Run the command-line below to ensure all the packages are available for selection:

```
$ make package/symlinks
```

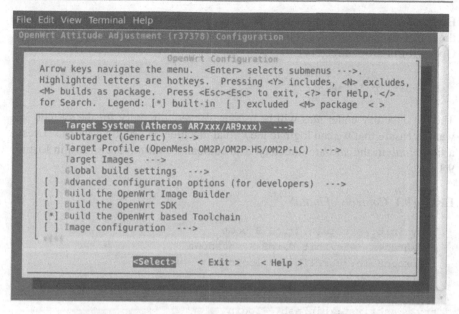

Fig. 9.1 Openwrt make menu

Openwrt is highly customisable and packages can be selected for inclusion through a menu driven configuration utility. Configure Openwrt with:

```
$ make menuconfig
```

The command above starts a menu based configuration utility as shown in Fig. 9.1. From the menu you can select the target system, which in our case is user mode Linux. Enter the Target System section and select:

```
(X) User Mode Linux
```

By default, the lightweight DNS/DHCP server dnsmasq is selected. As we do not want the system to run either DNS (or DHCP services), enter the Base section and locate the dnsmasq option. Unselect it:

```
< > dnsmasq
```

Another DHCP server application is also configured by default in the Network section. Enter the Network section and unselect odhcpd:

```
< > odhcpd...OpenWrt DHCP/DHCPv6(-PD)/RA Server & Relay
```

Exit and save from the configuration utility. Custom configuration files (such as those in /etc) can be defined at the build stage. Create a number of directories (in the Openwrt Buildroot directory):

```
$ mkdir -p files/etc
```

The *etc* directory under *files* will be used as the */etc* directory for the system. We want to ensure that we can login to the virtual machine on pseudo terminals. Create a file *inittab* in the *files/etc* directory. The contents of *inittab* are shown in Listing 9.1.

Listing 9.1 *Contents of inittab*

```
::sysinit:/etc/init.d/rcS S boot
::shutdown:/etc/init.d/rcS K shutdown
::askconsole:/usr/libexec/login.sh

# Start an "askfirst" shell on /dev/tty2-4
tty2::askfirst:/bin/ash --login
tty3::askfirst:/bin/ash --login
tty4::askfirst:/bin/ash --login
```

Build the firmware by running make:

```
$ make
```

The build can take a long time to complete. When it has completed, change to the parent directory (*openwrt_uml*) and copy the kernel and root filesystem to it:

```
$ cd ~/openwrt_uml
$ cp openwrt/bin/uml/openwrt-uml-vmlinux .
$ cp openwrt/bin/uml/openwrt-uml-ext4.img .
```

Make a symbolic link to the Linux kernel:

```
$ ln -s openwrt-uml-vmlinux linux
```

Create the UML launch script from Chap. 5 that is in Listing 5.4. Run the Openwrt UML virtual machine:

```
$ ./uml.sh -r openwrt-uml-ext4.img
```

The kernel boot process displays many lines of output to the screen. Towards the end of boot process, you will see lines like this:

```
Virtual console 2 assigned device '/dev/pts/15'
Virtual console 3 assigned device '/dev/pts/16'
Virtual console 4 assigned device '/dev/pts/18'
```

These are the pseudo terminals on which you can login. Start up a new terminal window and run minicom:

```
$ sudo minicom -D /dev/pts/15
```

You will see the Openwrt banner screen and the command-line prompt (you may have to hit the return key):

```
BusyBox v1.24.2 () built-in shell (ash)


  _____                      _____        __
 |       |.-----.-----.-----.|  |  |  |.----.|  |_
 |   -   ||  _  |  _  |  -__||  |  |  ||   _||   _|
 |_____||   __|_____|_____||_____||__|  |____|
          |__| W I R E L E S S   F R E E D O M
 -----------------------------------------------------
 DESIGNATED DRIVER (Bleeding Edge, 50108)
 -----------------------------------------------------
  * 2 oz. Orange Juice        Combine all juices in a
  * 2 oz. Pineapple Juice     tall glass filled with
  * 2 oz. Grapefruit Juice    ice, stir well.
  * 2 oz. Cranberry Juice
 -----------------------------------------------------
root@OpenWrt:/#
```

To stop the virtual machine gracefully, run:

```
root@OpenWrt:/# halt -d 5
```

We leave it to the reader to run this UML virtual machine with networking.

9.2 Open-mesh

In this section, we demonstrate building Openwrt for Open-Mesh OM2P devices [2]. The units are sold as WiFi mesh devices but can be reflashed with custom Openwrt firmware (see Fig. 9.2). Table 9.2 shows Open-Mesh OM2P and range as well as the OM1P unit, which has since been deprecated.

The build process for Open-mesh (or for any platform for that matter) is not dissimilar to the UML build above. Return to the Buildroot directory for Openwrt and run the configuration utility:

```
$ cd ~/openwrt_uml/openwrt
$ make menuconfig
```

The OM2P chipset is Atheros AR9285. Select the Target System menu item and then select the chipset:

```
(X) (X) Atheros AR7xxx/AR9xxx
```

If you have the legacy OM1P devices, which have the Atheros AR2315 chipset, then select the option Atheros AR231x/AR5312 Target System section. In this example, we use an OM2P-LC unit, therefore in the Target Profile we select the appropriate option:

Fig. 9.2 Open-mesh WiFi router

Table 9.2 Open-mesh models

Model	System type	CPU model	Speed (MHz)	Comment
OM1P	Atheros AR2315	MIPS 4KEc V6.4	183	Legacy hardware
OM2P	Atheros AR7240	MIPS 24Kc V7.4	400	
OM2P-LC	Atheros AT9330	MIPS 74Kc V4.12	400	Low-cost
OM2P-HS	Atheros AR9341	MIPS 24Kc V7.4	520	High-speed

```
(X) OpenMesh OM2P/OM2P-HS/OM2P-LC
```

The OM2P has watchdog hardware which will reboot the unit every five minutes if the timer is not reset. For this reason we select the om-watchdog option in the Base section:

```
<*> om-watchdog
```

The default SSH (secure shell) utility is Dropbear but Dropbear does not provide a secure FTP (SFTP) server. For this reason we install the OpenSSH server and SFTP server utilities. In the SSH subsection of the Network section, select openssh-server and openssh-sftp-server:

```
<*> openssh-server
<*> openssh-sftp-server
```

Next, create a *config* subdirectory under *files/etc*:

```
$ mkdir files/etc/config
```

The network interface configuration is specified in the host file directory *files/etc/config/network* in Listing 9.2.

Listing 9.2 *Contents of /etc/config/network*

```
config interface 'loopback'
option ifname 'lo'
option proto 'static'
option ipaddr '127.0.0.1'
option netmask '255.0.0.0'

config interface 'lan'
option ifname 'eth0'
option type 'bridge'
option proto 'static'
option ipaddr '172.16.50.236'
option gateway '172.16.50.1'
option netmask '255.255.255.0'
```

To compile the firmware image for the OM2P run the command below from the Buildroot directory:

```
$ make
```

This creates the firmware image in the directory *bin/ar71xx*. There are a number of files in this directory, but the one we are interested in is *openwrt-ar71xx-generic-om2p-squashfs-factory.bin*.
We need a utility (called ap51-flash) in order to flash the firmware onto the Open-mesh device. Download the source code:

```
$ svn co http://dev.cloudtrax.com/downloads/svn/\
> ap51-flash/trunk/ ap51-flash
```

Compile it:

```
$ pushd ap51-flash
~/ap51-flash ~
$ make
make -j 1 ap51-flash
make[1]: Entering directory '/home/aholt/ap51-flash'
    CC flash.o
    CC proto.o
    CC router_redboot.o
    CC router_tftp_client.o
    CC router_tftp_server.o
    CC router_types.o
    CC router_images.o
    CC socket.o
    CC commandline.o
    LD ap51-flash
strip ap51-flash
make[1]: Leaving directory '/home/aholt/ap51-flash'
$ popd
~
```

Connect the OM2P's Ethernet to your local switch but do *not* power on the OM2P at this point. Change to the *bin/atheros* subdirectory under the Buildroot directory and run ap51-flash to flash the firmware:

```
$ ~/ap51-flesh//ap51-flash eth0 \
> openwrt-ar71xx-generic-om2p-squashfs-factory.bin
```

Once the OM2P has booted up, we can Telnet to it and login as root without a password (at this stage):

```
$ telnet 169.254.105.57
root@OpenWrt:~/#
```

Set the root password:

```
root@OpenWrt:~/# passwd
```

Setting the password disables Telnet and enables SSH. Access to the device is now only through SSH (though your current Telnet session will continue until you log out). The default SSH utility is Dropbear but we prefer OpenSSH for its added functionality. We must first change the port that Dropbear listens on for SSH session:

```
root@OpenWrt:# uci set dropbear.@dropbear[0].Port=2022
root@OpenWrt:# uci commit dropbear
root@OpenWrt:# /etc/init.d/dropbear restart
```

We can now enable OpenSSH which will listen on SSH port 22:

```
root@OpenWrt:# /etc/init.d/sshd enable
root@OpenWrt:# /etc/init.d/sshd start
```

Remotely login using SSH and provide the root password when prompted:

```
$ ssh root@169.254.105.57
```

9.3 Dragino

In this section we discuss the Dragino MS14 (see Fig. 9.3) which, like Open-mesh, runs Openwrt. In the previous chapter we briefly introduced the Arduino micro-controller. The Arduino is not controlled by an operating system like GNU/Linux. Arduinos are pre-programmed with a bootloader for uploading user programs to the on-chip flash memory. User programs are compiled into an executable cyclic executive program.

The Arduino Yùn is a ATmega32u4 microcontroller which also incorporates an IEEE 802.11n SoC (system on a chip) for WiFi and Ethernet communication. The AR9331 SoC is a MIPS processor and runs Linino which is a customised version of Openwrt. The advantage of this configuration is that the GNU/Linux can be used to upload sketches to the ATmega32u5 remotely. Furthermore, sketches running on the ATmega32u4 can communicate with the GNU/Linux system. This makes it possible for sketches to run shell scripts and use the WiFi and Ethernet interfaces.

Like the Arduino Yùn, the Dragino MS14 is based upon a AR9331 SoC. It runs the Openwrt operating system, including the Arduino Yùn operating system, Linino. The Dragino does not come with a ATmega32u4 as standard but an ATmega32u processor is available as a plugin module, effectively, turning the Dragino MS14 into an Arduino Yùn. In this section we discuss the Dragino MS14 and the Arduino

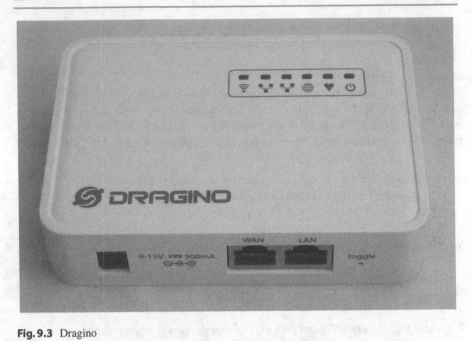

Fig. 9.3 Dragino

Fig. 9.4 The MS14-S (left) and MS14-P (right)

compatible plugin module, M32. There are two types of Dragino motherboard, the
MS14-S and and MS14-P. The difference between the two is that, the MS14-S has
an external terminal block so the GPIO ports can be accessed while motherboard is
in the casing (Fig. 9.4).

Fig. 9.5 M32 module

9.3.1 Booting up the Dragino for the First Time

The Dragino is shipped with an Openwrt operating system pre-installed. Power up the Dragino and connect the Ethernet port labelled "LAN" to the Ethernet port of a PC. The Dragino runs a DHCP service so the PC will bind to an IP address. If the PC does not receive any IP details automatically, issue the command (Fig. 9.5):

```
$ sudo dhclient eth0
```

Run a web browser and enter https://10.130.1.1/ into the URL dialogue box. This will display the initial login page shown in Fig. 9.6. As this is the first time the unit has booted up, the root password is not set. To set a password, click the text "Go to password configuration..." on the initial login page. The web page shown in Fig. 9.7 is displayed.

Enter a password in the password field (and in the confirmation field). Scroll down to the bottom of the screen and click "Save and Apply". Setting a root password will also enable an SSH service on the unit. We can now access the command-line of the unit remotely (when prompted for a password, use the one you set above):

```
$ ssh root@10.130.1.1
root@10.130.1.1's password:


BusyBox v1.19.4 (2013-09-17 16:18:02 CST) built-in shell
(ash)
Enter 'help' for a list of built-in commands.
```

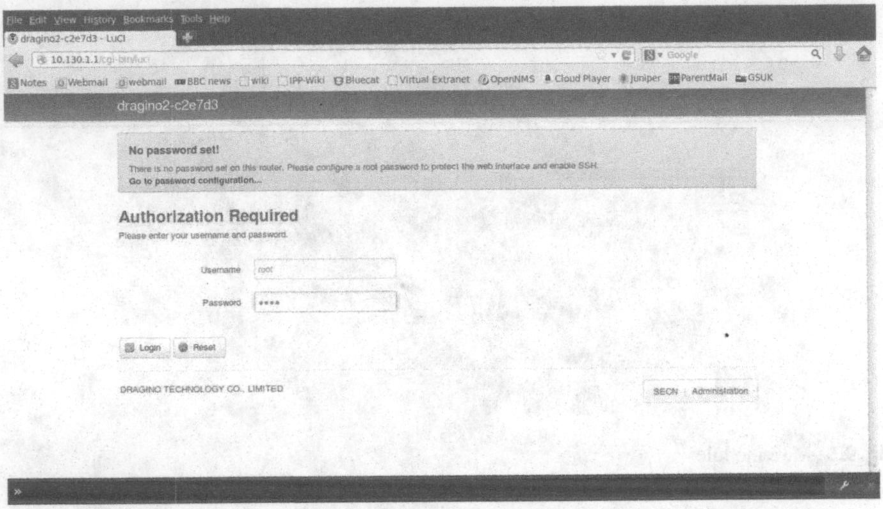

Fig. 9.6 Dragino login web page

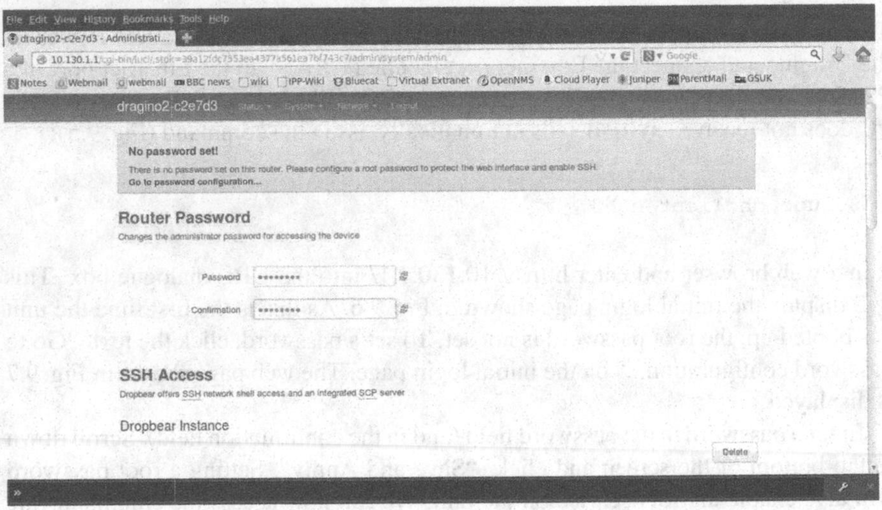

Fig. 9.7 Set the root password

```
 | \ |__\ |__| | _    | | | | |
 |__/ | | | | |__| _|_ | | | | |
----------------------------------------------
  W i F i ,  L i n u x ,  M C U ,  E m b e d d e d

Openwrt ATTITUDE ADJUSTMENT (r33887)
Dragino-v2 MS14 1.0-IoT-1
```

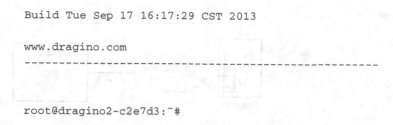

```
Build Tue Sep 17 16:17:29 CST 2013

www.dragino.com
-------------------------------------------------------



root@dragino2-c2e7d3:~#
```

9.3.2 Running Arduino Yùn Firmware

In this subsection we show how to reflash the Dragino with Linino version of Openwrt
which enables the Dragino to operate as Arduino Yùn. Unlike the Arduino Yùn,
the Dragino lacks a built-in ATmega32u4 processor. Instead, Dragino provides an
ATmega32u4 plugin module which can be programmed using the Arduino IDE.
Table 9.3 shows the technical specification for the M32 module.

The firmware can be downloaded from the web site in [3]. Click on the link for
the latest firmware. The kernel and root filesystem images are required:

- ms14-arduino-yun-kernel-beta1.3.bin
- ms14-arduino-yun-rootfs-squashfs-beta1.3.bin

The firmware is installed using TFTP (trivial file transfer protocol). Put the files above
into /tftpboot directory of TFTP server. The firmware is transferred to the Dragino by
initiating a TFTP download from the Dragino's bootloader prompt. The bootloader
prompt is accessible through the serial console. The Dragino's serial console can be

Table 9.3 M32 specification

Microcontroller	ATmega32u4
Operating voltage	5 V
I/O voltage	5 V
3.3 V output channel	1
5 V output channels	2
SRAM	2.5 KB
Flash memory	32 KB
EEPROM	1 KB
Clock speed	16 Mhz
Digital I/O pins	10
Analog input channels	8
PWM channels	4
ESD-protection	IEC 61000-4-2

Fig. 9.8 Arduino Yùn

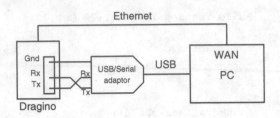

accessed using the UART_TX and UART_RX pins on the J1 block. We used a USB to serial converter to connect a PC to the Dragino serial port (if you do not have a USB/serial converter then an Arduino can be adapted, refer to Sect. 8.1.2). The TX pin of the USB/Serial converter is connected to the UART_RX pin of the Dragino. Similarly, connect the RX pin of the USB/Serial converter to the Dragino UART_TX pin.

We also connected the GND pins of the converter and Dragino. Figure 9.8 shows a diagram of the *crossover* console connection. We can now access the the serial console of the Dragino using a terminal emulator on the PC.

The diagram in Fig. 9.8 also shows the PC and Dragino connected via an Ethernet cable. We use the PC as a TFTP server from which the Dragino can download the firmware images.

Run the minicom terminal emulator:

```
$ sudo minicom -b 115200 -D /dev/ttyUSB0
```

The communication settings for the Dragino serial console are 115200 baud, 8 bits with no parity, so the terminal emulator should be configured accordingly. Power cycle the Dragino. Boot procedure messages are displayed on the console:

```
U-Boot 1.1.4 (Aug 12 2012 - 20:14:51)

AP121-2MB (ar9330) U-boot
DRAM:   #### TAP VALUE 1 = f, 2 = 10
64 MB
Top of RAM usable for U-Boot at: 84000000
Reserving 212k for U-Boot at: 83fc8000
Reserving 192k for malloc() at: 83f98000
Reserving 44 Bytes for Board Info at: 83f97fd4
Reserving 36 Bytes for Global Data at: 83f97fb0
Reserving 128k for boot params() at: 83f77fb0
Stack Pointer at: 83f77f98
Now running in RAM - U-Boot at: 83fc8000
id read 0x100000ff
flash size 16777216, sector count = 256
Flash: 16 MB
```

```
In:     serial
Out:    serial
Err:    serial
Net:    ag7240_enet_initialize...
No valid address in Flash. Using fixed address
No valid address in Flash. Using fixed address
: cfg1 0x5 cfg2 0x7114
eth0: 00:03:7f:09:0b:ad
eth0 up
: cfg1 0xf cfg2 0x7214
eth1: 00:03:7f:09:0b:ad
athrs26_reg_init_lan
ATHRS26: resetting s26
ATHRS26: s26 reset done
eth1 up
eth0, eth1
```

Interrupt the boot process when the line below is displayed. This needs to be done
within four seconds, otherwise, the boot process continues.

```
Hit any key to stop autoboot:   4
```

Interrupting the boot process drops you into the boot prompt:

```
dr_boot>
```

Initially, the Dragino has a default IP address of 192.168.255.1 (with 255.255.255.0
subnet mask). It expects the TFTP server to have an address of 192.168.255.2. Set
IP address of the TFTP server (which, in our case, is the PC in Fig. 9.8):

```
$ sudo ifconfig eth0 192.168.255.2 netmask \
> 255.255.255.0
```

From the boot prompt of the Dragino test the connectivity to the TFTP server:

```
dr_boot> ping 192.168.255.2
Using eth0 device
host 192.168.255.2 is alive
```

Upload the kernel image from the PC to the Dragino:

```
dr_boot> tftpboot 0x81000000 ms14-arduino-yun-kernel-bet
a1.3.bin
Using eth0 device
```

```
TFTP from server 192.168.255.2; our IP address is
192.168.255.1
Filename 'ms14-arduino-yun-kernel-beta1.3.bin'.
Load address: 0x81000000
Loading: #############################################
         #############################################
         #############################################
         ###################################
done
Bytes transferred = 1179648 (120000 hex)
```

Make a note of the bytes transferred (in this case 120000 hexadecimal). Now erase
a section of memory equal in size to the number of bytes transferred (note that the
last parameter is the number of bytes in hexadecimal that was transferred when the
kernel image was downloaded):

```
dr_boot> erase 0x9fea0000 +0x120000
Erase Flash from 0x9fea0000 to 0x9ffbffff in Bank # 1
First 0xea last 0xfb sector size 0x10000
 251
Erased 18 sectors
```

Copy the kernel to flash memory:

```
dr_boot> cp.b 0x81000000 0x9fea0000 $filesize
Copy to Flash... write addr: 9fea0000
done
```

Load the file containing the root filesystem (again making note of the number of
bytes transferred):

```
dr-boot> tftpboot 0x81000000  ms14-arduino-yun-rootfs-s
quashfs-beta1.3.bin
Using eth0 device
TFTP from server 192.168.255.2; our IP address is
192.168.255.1
Filename 'ms14-arduino-yun-rootfs-squashfs-beta1.3.bin'.
Load address: 0x81000000
Loading: #############################################
         #############################################
         #############################################
         #############################################
         #############################################
         #############################################
```

```
################################################
################################################
################################################
################################################
################################################
################################################
################################################
################################################
################################################
####################################
done
Bytes transferred = 5505024 (540000 hex)
```

Erase the flash memory (last parameter is the byte count of the file transfer above):

```
dr_boot> erase 0x9f050000 +0x540000
Erase Flash from 0x9f050000 to 0x9f58ffff in Bank # 1
First 0x5 last 0x58 sector size 0x10000
  88
Erased 84 sectors
```

Copy to flash:

```
dr_boot> cp.b 0x81000000 0x9f050000 $filesize
Copy to Flash... write addr: 9f050000
done
```

Set the boot address:

```
dr_boot> setenv bootcmd bootm 0x9fea0000
```

Save the environment:

```
dr_boot> saveenv
Saving Environment to Flash...
Protect off 9F030000 ... 9F03FFFF
Un-Protecting sectors 3..3 in bank 1
Un-Protected 1 sectors
Erasing Flash...Erase Flash from 0x9f030000 to
0x9f03ffff in Bank # 1
First 0x3 last 0x3 sector size 0x10000
  3
```

```
Erased 1 sectors
Writing to Flash... write addr: 9f030000
done
Protecting sectors 3..3 in bank 1
Protected 1 sectors
```

Reboot the unit:

```
dr_boot> reset
```

The Dragino will reboot but on this occasion do not interrupt the boot process.
Once the operating system has booted, it will broadcast and open SSID with a prefix
"Dragino-" followed by a sequence of hexadecimal digits. Our unit, for example, has
the SSID Dragino-A84041134E3C. In order to test the unit, associate with the SSID
then SSH to the root account of the unit (the default root password is "arduino"):

```
$ ssh root@192.168.240.1
root@192.168.240.1's password:


BusyBox v1.19.4 (2014-04-15 14:13:15 CST) built-in
shell (ash)
Enter 'help' for a list of built-in commands.
```

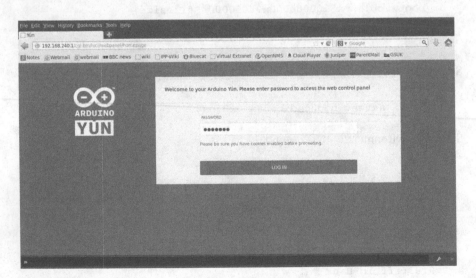

Fig. 9.9 Arduino login page

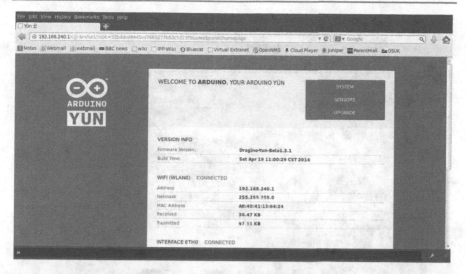

Fig. 9.10 Arduino Yùn Welcome page

```
Firmware Version: Dragino-Yun-Beta1.3.1
Build Sat Apr 19 11:00:29 CST 2014

root@Arduino:~#
```

The Dragino can also be accessed using a web browser using the URL: http://192.
168.240.1/. Figure 9.9 shows the web login page. Enter "Arduino" into the password
dialogue box and click the "LOG IN" button. This takes you to the Arduino Yùn
welcome page (Fig. 9.10).

9.4 Programming the M32 Unit

The M32 unit is an Arduino compatible plugin unit for the Dragino. The M32 con-
nects to the MS14 using the J1 and J5 expansion headers. Figure 9.11 shows the M32
modules plugged into the expansion headers of the Dragino Motherboard. Run the
Arduino IDE and enter the sketch in Listing 9.3. This is a simple sketch that blinks
an LED connected to Dragino's pin 2 (which is actually pin 4 on terminal block).
(see Sect. 8.1 for instructions on how to install the Arduino IDE).

Fig. 9.11 The M32 module attached the Dragino motherboard

Listing 9.3 *Arduino Sketch for blinking an LED*

```
/*
  Flash led on pin 2
*/

int led = 2;

void setup() {
  pinMode(led, OUTPUT);
}

void loop() {
  digitalWrite(led, HIGH);
  delay(200);
  digitalWrite(led, LOW);
  delay(200);
}
```

Before compiling the sketch, the Arduino board type and port needs to set. To set
the board type, select "Tools" and then select "Board" from the drop down menu.
Another drop down menu appears with a selection of Arduino board types. Select

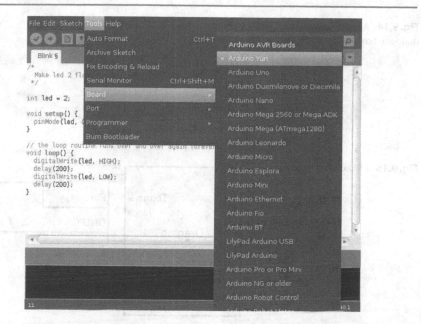

Fig. 9.12 Set the Arduino board type

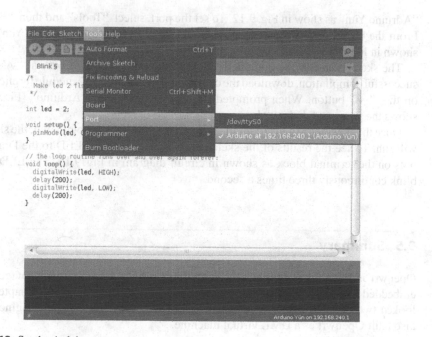

Fig. 9.13 Set the Arduino port

Fig. 9.14 Arduino password
dialogue box

Fig. 9.15 LED circuit

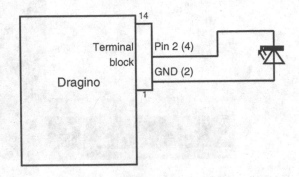

"Adruino Yùn" as show in Fig. 9.12. To set the port, select "Tools" and then "Port".
From the drop down menu select "Arduino at 192.168.240.1 (Arduino Yùn)" as
shown in Fig. 9.13.

The sketch can now be compiled, click on the button marked with a "√". On
successful compilation, download the compiled sketch to the M32 module by clicking
on the "→" button. When prompted for a password, enter "Arduino" (Fig. 9.14
shows the password dialogue box).

Once the download of the (compiled) sketch to the M32 has completed, the sketch
will run. To see the results of the sketch execution, connect an LED to the Dragino
pins on the terminal block as shown in circuit diagram in Fig. 9.15. The LED will
blink continuously three times a second.

9.5   Summary

Openwrt is a complete framework for building GNU/Linux firmware images for
embedded systems. Openwrt is available for many platforms. In this chapter we
looked two devices, namely, the Open-mesh OMxP devices and the Dragino. We
also built Openwrt as a UML virtual machine.

The Open-mesh is sold as a WiFi mesh solution but its firmware can be reflashed with a custom Openwrt operating system.

The Dragino can also be reflashed with custom Openwrt firmware. The interesting feature of the Dragino is that it can run the Linino which is the custom firmware for the Arduino Yûn.

References

1. OpenWRT (2013) OpenWRT table of hardware, http://wiki.openwrt.org/toh/start. Accessed 21 June 2013
2. Open mesh UK (2013) Open mesh, http://www.openmesh-uk.com/. Accessed 4 Jan 2013
3. Dragino (2014) Yun firmware download, http://www.dragino.com/downloads/index.php?dir=motherboards/ms14/Firmware/Yun/. Accessed 16 June 2014

Udhcpd Default Script

A

This Appendices lists the contents of the */usr/share/udhcpc/default.script* file.

Listing A.1 *Content of /usr/share/udhcpc/default.script*

```
#!/bin/sh

[ -z "$1" ] && echo "Error: call from udhcpc only" && exit 1

RESOLV_CONF="/etc/resolv.conf"
RESOLV_BAK="/etc/resolv.bak"

[ -n "$broadcast" ] && BROADCAST="broadcast $broadcast"
[ -n "$subnet" ] && NETMASK="netmask $subnet"

case "$1" in
    deconfig)
        if [ -f "$RESOLV_BAK" ]; then
            mv "$RESOLV_BAK" "$RESOLV_CONF"
        fi
        /sbin/ifconfig $interface 0.0.0.0
        ;;

    renew|bound)
        /sbin/ifconfig $interface $ip $BROADCAST $NETMASK

        if [ -n "$router" ]
        then
            for i in $router ; do
                route add default gw $i dev $interface
            done
        fi

        if [ ! -f "$RESOLV_BAK" ] && [ -f "$RESOLV_CONF" ]
        then
```

© Springer International Publishing AG, part of Springer Nature 2018
A. Holt and C.-Y. Huang, *Embedded Operating Systems*, Undergraduate
Topics in Computer Science, https://doi.org/10.1007/978-3-319-72977-0

```
            mv "$RESOLV_CONF" "$RESOLV_BAK"
        fi

        if [ ! -f "$RESOLV_BAK" ] && [ -f "$RESOLV_CONF" ]
        then
            mv "$RESOLV_CONF" "$RESOLV_BAK"
        fi

        echo -n > $RESOLV_CONF
        [ -n "$domain" ] && echo search $domain >> $RESOLV_CONF
        for i in $dns ; do
            echo nameserver $i >> $RESOLV_CONF
        done
        ;;
esac

exit 0
```

Start-up Scripts

B

The start-up/shutdown scripts for Sect. 6.3 are listed in this Appendix. These files need to be created in the *$ROOT/etc/init.d* directory.

Listing B.1 *Contents of /etc/init.d/rc.S*

```
#!/bin/sh

PATH=/sbin:/bin/:/usr/sbin:/usr/bin
runlevel=S
prevlevel=N
umask 022
export PATH runlevel prevlevel

# Read configuration variables
[ -f /etc/defaults/rcS ] && . /etc/defaults/rcS
export VERBOSE

trap ":" INT QUIT TSTP

for i in /etc/rcS.d/S??*
do
        # Ignore dangling symlinks
        [ ! -f "$i" ] && continue
        case "$i" in
                *.sh)
                        (
                                trap - INT QUIT TSTP
                                set start
                                . $i
                        )
                        ;;
                *)
                        $i start
                        ;;
```

© Springer International Publishing AG, part of Springer Nature 2018
A. Holt and C.-Y. Huang, *Embedded Operating Systems*, Undergraduate
Topics in Computer Science, https://doi.org/10.1007/978-3-319-72977-0

```
        esac
done
```

Listing B.2 *Contents of* /etc/init.d/rc

```
#!/bin/sh

for i in /etc/rc${1}.d/K*; do
        [ ! -f $i ] && continue
        case "$i" in
                *.sh)
                                sh $i stop
                                ;;
                *)
                                $i stop
                                ;;
        esac
done

for i in /etc/rc${1}.d/S*; do
        [ ! -f $i ] && continue
        case "$i" in
                *.sh)
                                sh $i start
                                ;;
                *)
                                $i start
                                ;;
        esac
done
```

Listing B.3 *Contents of* /etc/init.d/mountall

```
#!/bin/sh

case $1 in
        start|"")
                        /bin/mount -na
                        /bin/mount -n -o remount,rw /
                        ;;
        stop)
                        /bin/umount -na
                        ;;
        *)        echo "Usage: mountall [start|stop]" >&2
                        exit 3
                        ;;
esac
```

Listing B.4 shows the bootmisc script.

Listing B.4 *Contents of* /etc/init.d/bootmisc

```
#!/bin/sh

start_up () {

        # Create /var directory
        tar xf /var.tar

        # Save dmesg output
        /bin/dmesg >/var/log/dmesg

        # Create FIFO
        [ ! -p /dev/initctl ] && /usr/bin/mkfifo /dev/initctl

        # Create /var/run/utmp
        touch /var/run/utmp

}

case "$1" in
  start|"")
        start_up
        ;;
  stop)
        # No operation
        ;;
  *)
        echo "Usage: bootmisc [start|stop]" >&2
        exit 3
        ;;
esac
```

Listing B.5 *Contents of* /etc/init.d/hostname

```
#!/bin/sh

if [ -f /etc/hostname ] then
        /bin/hostname -F /etc/hostname
fi
```

Listing B.6 *Contents of* /etc/init.d/network

```
#!/bin/sh

case "$1" in
```

```
        start)
                echo -n "Bring up network interfaces: "
                /sbin/ifup -a
                echo "done."
                ;;
        stop)
                echo -n "Take down network interfaces: "
                /sbin/ifdown -a
                echo "done."
                ;;
        force-reload|restart)
                echo -n "Reconfigure network interfaces: "
                ifdown -a
                ifup -a
                echo "done."
                ;;
esac
```

Listing B.7 *Contents of* /etc/init.d/syslogd

```
#!/bin/sh

UNAME=syslogd
UTIL=/sbin/${UNAME}
DESC=${UNAME}

if [ ! -x ${UTIL} ]; then
        echo Skipping ${DESC}.
        exit 2
fi

set -e

case "$1" in
        start)
                echo -n "Starting ${UNAME}: "
                ${UTIL}
                EXIT=$?
                if [ $EXIT == 0 ]; then
                        echo "${UNAME} started sucessfully."
                else
                        echo "${UNAME} failed."
                fi
                ;;
        stop)
                echo -n "Stopping ${UNAME}: "
                if killall ${UNAME}
                then
                        echo "${UNAME} stopped sucessfully."
                else
                        echo "${UNAME} failed."
                fi
```

```
                    ;;
        *)
                echo "usage: $0 {start|stop}"
                exit 1;
esac

exit 0
```

Listing B.8 *Contents of* /etc/init.d/klogd

```
#!/bin/sh

UNAME=klogd
UTIL=/sbin/${UNAME}
DESC=${UNAME}

if [ ! -x ${UTIL} ]; then
        echo Skipping ${DESC}.
        exit 2
fi

set -e

case "$1" in
        start)
                echo -n "Starting ${UNAME}: "
                ${UTIL}
                EXIT=$?
                if [ $EXIT == 0 ]; then
                        echo "${UNAME} started sucessfully."
                else
                        echo "${UNAME} failed."
                fi
                ;;
        stop)
                echo -n "Stopping ${UNAME}: "
                if killall ${UNAME}
                then
                        echo "${UNAME} stopped sucessfully."
                else
                        echo "${UNAME} failed."
                fi
                ;;
        *)
                echo "usage: $0 {start|stop}"
                exit 1;
esac

exit 0
```

Listing B.9 *Contents of* /etc/init.d/telnet

```
#!/bin/sh

UNAME=telnetd
UTIL=/usr/sbin/${UNAME}
DESC="Telnet daemon"

if [ ! -x ${UTIL} ]; then
        echo Skipping ${DESC}.
        exit 2
fi

set -e

case "$1" in
        start)
                echo -n "Starting ${UNAME}: "
                ${UTIL}
                EXIT=$?
                if [ $EXIT == 0 ]; then
                        echo "${UNAME} started sucessfully."
                else
                        echo "${UNAME} failed."
                fi
                ;;
        stop)
                echo -n "Stopping ${UNAME}: "
                if killall ${UNAME}
                then
                        echo "${UNAME} stopped sucessfully."
                else
                        echo "${UNAME} failed."
                fi
                ;;
        *)
                echo "usage: $0 {start|stop}"
                exit 1;
esac

exit 0
```

Listing B.10 *Contents of* /etc/init.d/ntp

```
#!/bin/sh

UNAME=ntpd
UTIL=/usr/sbin/${UNAME}
DESC="NTP daemon"
RTC=/sbin/hwclock
```

```
SERVER=0.debian.pool.ntp.org

if [ ! -x ${UTIL} ]; then
        echo Skipping ${DESC}.
        ${RTC} -s    # set system clock from RTC
        exit 2
fi

set -e

case "$1" in
        start)
                echo -n "Starting ${UNAME}: "
                ${UTIL} -p ${SERVER}
                EXIT=$?
                if [ $EXIT == 0 ]; then
                        echo "${UNAME} started sucessfully."
                else
                        echo "${UNAME} failed."
                fi
                ;;
        stop)
                echo -n "Stopping ${UNAME}: "
                $RTC -w    # sync RTC with system clock
                if killall ${UNAME}
                then
                        echo "${UNAME} stopped sucessfully."
                else
                        echo "${UNAME} failed."
                fi
                ;;
        *)
                echo "usage: $0 {start|stop}"
                exit 1;
esac

exit 0
```

Listing B.11 *Contents of* /etc/init.d/halt

```
#!/bin/sh

echo -n "Halting... "
/sbin/halt -d2  -f
```

Listing B.12 *Contents of* /etc/init.d/reboot

```
#!/bin/sh

echo -n "Rebooting... "
/sbin/reboot -d2 -f
```

Glossary

API	Application programming interface
Bash	Bourne again shell—a command-line interpretter
Busybox	A collection of Unix utilities designed for embedded systems
COTS	Commercial off the shelf
Debian	A GNU/Linux distribution
GCC	GNU compiler collection
Glibc	GNU C Library
GNU	GNU is not Unix
Grub	Grand unified bootloader
Ncurses	A library of screen handling functions
NSS	Name switch service
SDN	Software defined networks
TCP/IP	Transmission control protocol/internet protocol
Tmpfs	Temporary file system
Ubuntu	A GNU/Linux distribution based upon Debian
UML	User mode Linux
Vi	A text editor
VM	Virtual machine

© Springer International Publishing AG, part of Springer Nature 2018
A. Holt and C.-Y. Huang, *Embedded Operating Systems*, Undergraduate
Topics in Computer Science, https://doi.org/10.1007/978-3-319-72977-0

Index

© Springer International Publishing AG, part of Springer Nature 2018
A. Holt and C.-Y. Huang, *Embedded Operating Systems*, Undergraduate
Topics in Computer Science, https://doi.org/10.1007/978-3-319-72977-0